The Girlfriend's Guide to FOOTBALL

THE Girlfriend's GUIDE TO FOOTBALL

by Teena Spencer

WITH CHUCK BROWN

FIREFLY BOOKS

A FIREFLY BOOK

Published by Firefly Books (U.S.) Inc. 2001

First Printing

U.S. Cataloguing-in-Publication Data
(Library of Congress Standards)

Spencer, Teena.
    The girlfriend's guide to football / Teena Spencer ;
        with Chuck Brown.– 1st ed.
[192] p. : col. ill. ; cm.
ISBN 1-55209-608-4 (pbk.)
Football. II. Brown, Chuck III. Title.
796.962 21   2001   CIP

Published in the United States in 2001 by
Firefly Books (U.S.) Inc.
P.O. Box 1338, Ellicott Station
Buffalo, New York, USA
14205

Published in Canada in 2001 by Key Porter Books Limited.

Design and Electronic formatting: Lightfoot Art & Design Inc.

Printed and bound in Canada

Contents

Introduction

JUST ONE OF THE GUYS

Football has traditionally been a male domain—from the fans to the players to the coaches, "a guy thing." But the last few years have seen a surprising demographic shift. More women than ever are watching—and playing—football. The National Football League (NFL) estimates that currently 43 percent of its total fan base is female.

It's true, and I should know. I'm one of those newly drafted female fans.

My passion for football didn't light up the sky immediately. I had a healthy hatred for the game to overcome first.

The great coach Vince Lombardi once said, "Football is a great deal like life in that it teaches you that work, sacrifice, perseverance, competitive drive, selflessness, and respect for authority is the price that each and every one of us must pay to achieve any goal that is worthwhile."

My little sister Tricia Dickerson once said, "Football is stupid; let's go wax our legs." I agreed with my sister.

My hatred for the game was still strong when football season struck last year and turned all my once close and easy to talk to male friends into idiots who spoke an incomprehensible language.

"Warner's calling an audible from the shotgun, he's got his wide-out in motion, and here comes the safety blitz!" Huh?

I was horrified. I felt betrayed. Football had stolen my boys and I liked my boys. I mean, I *really* liked my boys. I liked going out, hanging out, and shootin' the proverbial poop with the guys. I think that they're funny, goofy, and generally great company. But invariably in any funny, goofy, great conversation sports come up. Soccer—no problem, I played in high school. Hockey—bring it on, I already wrote the book. Football—who wants another beer?

Ever since I wrote about hockey in my first *Girlfriend's Guide*, men love talking about the game with me. At first, some guys had a hard time believing that I was actually a fan and would challenge me. After hours of "hockey talk" and proving my true patriotism by naming the year that the Maple Leafs last won the Cup (1967, if anyone asks), they would finally believe that I knew what the heck I was talking about. Hockey became a cinch, and I not only participated in hockey round-tables with the guys, but I led the conversations and won "friendly"debates with my buddies. But when the conversation turned to football, I turned into "Teena-the-frozen-lipped-beer-fetcher." While the guys frothed at the mouth at the mere mention of the Super Bowl, I was Super Bored. Eventually, I decided that I would watch a game just to see what all the fuss was about.

After watching my inaugural game of football, two thoughts struck me (which I'm sure others have had): "What the hell is going on?"and "Holy cow! Is that guy dead?" Frankly, the game terrified me. Men who looked as if they weighed about a thousand pounds collided in midair with other men who looked as if they weighed a thousand pounds. Then, every once in a while, all the players would decide to jump on one poor bastard. This poor bastard would then be squashed under a heap of blubbery bods. Miraculously, when all the hulking players had righted themselves, the poor bastard walked away (usu-ally). But the violent acrobatics scared the bejesus out of me, and as if that wasn't enough, the game was mind-numbingly slow. The teams didn't actually seem to move, and each game seemed to last longer than the Jurassic Period. (Don't get me started on the bimbos bouncing their boobies on the sidelines.) Above all, though, the game itself was so confusing that it drove me insane. After watching a few games, I decided to stick to beer-fetching during football talk.

And then the boys started jabbering about the Super Bowl. It was early in the season, but the closer the Super Bowl got, the more excited they became. Just like every year, they nearly whipped themselves into a frenzy, driving me nuts with their incomprehensible football chatter. After listening to these yahoos for years, I decided that I'd finally had enough. It was time to make a decision: either hide out at home every weekend for the next few months and wax my legs with my sister or learn the game of football.

In this open frame of mind, I set out to teach myself the basics, but I was soon disappointed. There were no books that explained the rudi-ments of the game in a language that the average uninitiated adult—or a woman with a mission—could understand. But, like those tough guys I saw on television, I persisted. And after wading through dozens of bulky football encyclopedias, watching countless games, and faithfully reading the sports pages, I slowly began to understand how football works. I also enlisted the help of my buddy Chuck Brown, a writer and official football guy. Chuck and I often got together over a few brewskies to watch the game and lay a few friend-ly wagers on the outcome (until his wife busted us). I usually won, of course.

> **Chuck:**
> She lies! She lies like a cheap rug. She lost every bet and will go down in football history as the world's worst football bettor. Um, even though betting is wrong and I never do it anymore.

Although Chuck cheated when we bet, he proved to be invaluable in help-ing me to understand the game. He had all the answers, from "What are those things on their noses?" to "Can you lend me twenty bucks? I bet that big guy over there that the Bears would win." I'm sure you'll enjoy his commentary throughout this book as much as I have through-out my football journey. You will also notice that Chuck and I mostly focus on the NFL. Why? Because I'm sure your football guy yacks about it constantly. But just in case your guy babbles about the Canadian Football League (CFL) or the U.S. college game, we've got you covered and included chapters on them as well.

So, what did I find out? Why do guys like football? Hmmmm… let me see. The players wear skintight pants. They pat each other's incred-ibly tight butts a lot. They run and jump and sweat. The quarterback usually has perfect teeth and is able to smile through the pain as he limps off the field after making the game-winning pass. And the hand-some players are stinkin' filthy rich. Why do guys like football? Who cares! I know why I like football.

I mean, there are other reasons for watching the game, those are just the best ones. Aside from form-fitting uniforms and pearly teethed, ball-slingin' studs, football is a war waged by men of skill, courage, and determination (and hard, squeezable asses). When you first watch a game, you'll probably see twenty-two guys smashing into one anoth-er and then lining up to do it again. But when you learn the game, as I have, you'll start to see the real game, the game that us girls have been missing out on for too long. Those guys do smash into each other (and it's pretty cool when they do), but when you know a little bit about football, you'll learn to appreciate why they are doing it. In football, there is plenty of brawn, but the game also requires a lot of brains, too. There are strategies involved in moving that weird ball around the field. The players must memorize a playbook that weighs as much as a Volkswagen, and then execute the plays perfectly when asked.

Football is colorful, it's loud, and it's exciting. The players come in all shapes and sizes, each with his own special skill (and rock-hard tushie). Most NFL games are telecast on the most boring of all days—Sunday—so this gives you an excuse to either laze on the couch all day or go out for excessive beer and wings. Generally, the rest of the NFL games are on *Monday Night Football*, a good time to refine that couch-lazin' or recover from Sunday's hot wing hangover.

So, why do guys like football? Hot, rich players shaking their tight booties… speed, grace, courage, and shiny pants. You know, I have no idea.

Whose bright idea was this anyway?

THE ORIGINS OF THE GAME

Evolution, Not Invention

Football's history is almost as complex as the game itself. Wouldn't it have been great if some guy named Earl had just woken up one morning and created a new sport with an egg-shaped ball and eleven angry men on each side trying to take that ball into the other team's end zone? Sadly, there was no Earl and hence there is no easy explanation for the madness we see on TV every Sunday from September to January. But if you read this chapter, I guarantee you'll know more than a whole stadium full of Buffalo Bills fans.

OFF WITH HIS HEAD!

A few fanciful (and questionable) stories exist about the origins of football. One of the best ones involves those pesky Vikings.

One day in the eighth century, a bunch of innocent men were sitting upon the shores of old mother England. Suddenly, a gaggle of ships showed up filled with snarling Vikings. The Vikings stormed ashore, hurling spears and strange-sounding insults. The innocent English men, who wanted little more than a good cup of tea and a nice sheep innards pie, kicked the Vikings' butts and captured their leader. The English decided to chop off the Viking leader's head and began kicking it around. The English boys discovered that this game was "Jolly good fun, lads," and football was born.

Sounds a little fishy to me. It is hard to believe that those sissy, pram-pushin', bubble-and-squeak-munchin', crooked-teethed pansies could beat anybody, let alone crazed, hairy Vikings.

And, of course, the story doesn't end there. Since those disgusting Brits didn't have a human head to kick about every day (it was hard to get good Viking heads in those days—they only last so long), an alternative had to be invented. Since they were disgusting Brits, they cut the bladder out of a dead cow, dried the bladder out in the sun, and blew it up. Unfortunately, the bladders weren't as tough as a Viking's head (there's a surprise), so they began wrapping the bladders in animal skin for protection. The skin of a pig proved to be the best for the job, and the rest is history—a kind of I-don't-think-I-believe-this-crap history, but still history nonetheless.

SOCCER'S BASTARD CHILD

Seriously, the game of football evolved from rugby in the mid-nineteenth century. But, in the beginning, there was soccer. A simple game. An athletic pursuit. A gentlemanly way to partake in a little healthy competition. Kicking balls around has always been a popular pursuit among men and has existed for two thousand years.

Chuck:
My legs are crossed.

Throughout the world, except in North America, soccer is known as football—some quaint men with accents even refer to it as "footy," which is not to be confused with "footsies." Soccer, football, or whatever you want to call it, is a kicking game, and it's the most popular sport in the world.

Americans, too, have always loved their ball-kicking, and university boys used to play soccer to help unwind from the stress of their studies. They pursued other athletic endeavors, too—things like drinking, wrestling, drinking, fighting, and drinking. Everyone played the game of soccer, and everyone agreed that it was the best game in town. Then came along a little bugger named William Webb Ellis. Ellis played soccer at Rugby College in England in 1823. One day, in extreme frustration, Ellis picked up the soccer ball and ran. Ellis outraged many by flagrantly cheating (as opposed to unflagrantly cheating), but he also became a hero to young rebels everywhere. Soon other players began to play a new game that evolved from Ellis's little stunt. The new game was called rugby, named after the college where it was first invented. William Webb Ellis's refusal to follow the mainstream earned him cult-hero status, and eventually a plaque honoring his achievement was hung at Rugby College.

Thanks to British colonialism, both soccer and rugby were huge sports in most of the world back in the 1800s. Rugby was a rough and tough game; so rough, in fact, that it was banned at Harvard in 1860.

The First Game of Football

The first intercollegiate football game in the U.S. was played on November 6, 1869, between New Jersey schools Rutgers and Princeton. It was just a tad different from our modern game of football, in that there were twenty-five players on each side and the players advanced the ball by butting it with their heads. They could also kick it, of course. There were no touchdowns, field goals, or conversion points (see the Glossary on page 174 for definitions of these terms), and goals were scored by kicking the ball between goalposts that were twenty-five yards apart. The first team to get six goals won. The game they were actually playing was closer to soccer than our version of football. Nonetheless, Rutgers beat Princeton 6–4, then Princeton won the rematch a week later. Must be the appeal of head-butting a ball, but other schools jumped on the bandwagon and formed teams—first Columbia in 1870, then Yale in 1872.

Despite the 1860 ban on rugby, those wimps at Harvard were back playing a rugby-style game when they were convinced by Yale to try something different. In 1875, the two teams met and played a football-style game where touchdowns were worth a point, a conversion kick counted for four, and a field goal was worth five.

The Rules are Written

Remember the kid next door when you were little? The one that made up the rules to his stupid games as he went along? That was kind of what football was like in the early days. Eventually, some general rules had to be defined and accepted. This is the story of how the rules came to be.

WHO'S TO BLAME?

Walter Camp—if anyone's to blame for this mess, it's him. In the beginning, football was in a state of chaos. Everyone had different rules and there really was no one game that players everywhere could comprehend. Then a sensational player at Yale named Walter Camp stepped in and, in 1876, the first rules of football were written and accepted at the

Massasoit Convention by the Intercollegiate Football Association (the forerunner of the National Collegiate Athletic Association, known as the NCAA). The original rules were actually for a game that was closer to soccer and rugby rather than the game we know today, but they continued to evolve from that day forward, like this:

Group Hug, Boys: In 1877, football was a love-in—with more bleeding. The players got to know each other intimately, with players on both teams clustering around the ball and kicking at it to drive it free. When it eventually popped loose, a player picked it up and ran for his life. When he met up with the opposition, he either kicked the ball away or passed it laterally or backward to a teammate.

A Line in the Sand: In 1880, Walter Camp had a wild and crazy idea—alternate possessions. He thought that each team should have a turn with the ball. The rules convention okayed the idea and the line of scrimmage was invented to define the offense and defense (those with the ball and those without.)

Eleven's Company, Fifteen's a Crowd: In 1880, the rules committee also dropped the number of players per side from fifteen to eleven. That number has stuck and remains the NFL standard.

Holy Snappin' Armpits: The year 1880 was big in football's development. Another change to the game resulted in the creation of the "quarterback" who took the ball from the "snapper," now called the "center." Initially, the snapper could hike the ball to the quarterback using only his foot; later, he was allowed to guide the ball with his hands. Today, the center is allowed to snap the ball with both hands, and he and the quarterback have a special relationship that appears to fall just short of a full rectal probe.

Dumb It down a Bit: During the next couple of years, Walter Camp came up with a few more brilliant football ideas. The sensational captain of the Yale team was the first to have his quarterback call plays. Today's quarterbacks might yell out something like "Red 93! Blue 29! Six–three–nine post swing on two!" Early quarterbacks, however, called plays like "Okay Bob, we're going to kick it now!"

Once the line of scrimmage was established, teams developed blocking strategies to protect their quarterbacks and open room for runners. One team kept the ball for the whole first half and the other team took it for the second half. Then Camp had another bright idea: the offensive team would be given three tries to make five yards. If they failed, the other team got the ball.

He Kicks, He Scores: In 1883, Camp created a standardized scoring system that was heavy on the hoofing. Kicking a field goal (when the player kicks the ball through the goalposts) was now worth five points and a conversion kick (extra points given for kicking the ball through the goalposts after a touchdown) was worth four. Touchdowns were worth a measly two.

Death and Destruction: In 1888, a rule was created that allowed tackling to occur as low as the knees. Carnage and mayhem ensued. Runners went down and never got back up. The offense bunched up around the runner and formed a wedge to cut through the defense. The game was brutal; fighting became part of the mayhem. In 1905, eighteen players died and 159 were seriously injured. The destruction led to a White House conference and the creation of the NCAA to oversee the game.

Touchdown's Stock Rises: In 1892, a touchdown grew to be worth four points and a conversion kick was changed to two points. Protective equipment was still scarce in 1892, and players played the full ninety minutes unless their sorry carcasses had to be dragged from the field. In 1897, a touchdown was bumped up to five points and the conversion kick (also known as the "point after touchdown" or extra point) went down to one.

Are You Making a Forward Pass at Me? In 1906, the forward pass was legalized, but it didn't have an immediate impact. A pass could travel no farther than twenty yards and an incomplete pass resulted in a fifteen-yard loss. Forward passes were too risky for most chuckers to attempt.

More Ch-Ch-Changes: In the early 1900s, the games were shortened from seventy to sixty minutes, and five yards no longer cut it for a first down—you had to get ten yards. A neutral zone was set up between the teams on the line of scrimmage to give them a little breathing room, and a rule required the offense to have six players on the line. That eliminated plays where blockers would take a running start and hit the scrimmage line with a head of steam. In 1910, the rules required seven blockers on the line.

A Pro is Born

The birth of professional sports in America developed after the Civil War (1861–65), when outdoor activities such as golfing and bicycling became popular. Shortly afterward, in 1868, the first athletic club was formed in New York. By 1871, baseball was a professional sport, but the Amateur Athletic Union fought to stop the practice, calling pro athletes "tramps" and "opportunists" who sold their services to colleges and athletic clubs. Athletic clubs fought back, however, and in 1889, six clubs formed a union of their own. These clubs—Baltimore, Boston, New Jersey, and three different New York clubs—fought each year for the amateur title of America. As the competition became fierce, clubs pursued the best athletes. The Amateur Athletic Union battled professionalism in sports, but players were soon getting paid in roundabout, sneaky ways so that it was difficult to trace their salaries. For example, a football club could award a gold watch to an athlete as a prize. The player would take the watch to a pawnshop and sell it for $20. Then he'd go back to the club manager or promoter and sell him the pawn ticket for another $20. The promoter would then go back to the pawnshop and retrieve the watch for another $20. And the trophy for the next game… was the exact same watch. To stop the madness, the Amateur Athletic Union ruled that trophies could no longer be awarded and limited gifts or prizes to banners worth 25¢. However, big athletic clubs still bucked the rules by handing out travel expenses worth double the actual travel costs.

Here are a few highlights of professional football's development.

First Ringer: On November 12, 1892, William "Pudge" Heffelfinger was paid $500 under the table by a club in Pittsburgh and became the first-ever documented professional football player.

Modern Times: Something similar to the modern Sunday madness began to take shape in 1912 when touchdowns went up to six points and field goals down to three. The field also shrank to 100 yards from 110 yards, and the offense was given four cracks at making ten yards.

Yo, Rockne! Football players finally figured out how to make a pass in 1913, when Notre Dame quarterback Gus Dorais and end Knute Rockne practiced the seldom-used tactic. Rockne clued in that the forward pass—which was legal but almost never used—might work better if he caught the ball on the run instead of standing there waiting for it. Dorais and Rockne debuted their new weapon the next season and managed to upset the heavily favored Army team 35–13. Dorais completed seventeen of twenty-four passes while the Army boys watched in slack-jawed awe. The forward pass was now an integral part of the game.

A League Is Born: On September 17, 1920, in Canton, Ohio, the American Professional Football Association was founded. A membership fee of $100 was required, although no team ever paid it. After the 1921 season, the league's name was officially changed to the National Football League.

Big "Red": In 1925, all-American halfback Harold "Red" Grange signed a contract to play for the Chicago Bears, a team that had recently sucked. On Thanksgiving Day of that year, 36,000 fans (the biggest crowd in early football history) showed up to watch Red play. A short while later, on New York's Polo Grounds, Red drew more than 73,000 fans for a game against the New York Giants. Red soon became known as the "Galloping Ghost" and was football's first crowd-drawing superstud.

Who's the Best: The new NFL didn't have a playoff system to decide its champion until 1932. Before that year, the championship award was based on a vote at league meetings. In 1933, the NFL divided into two divisions. The top team from each division battled for the championship. As unfair as it seems, it wasn't until 1936 that every team in the league played the same number of games.

The Old Guard: Only two teams that exist today started with the original league in 1920: the Chicago Bears (who began life as the Decatur Staleys) and the Chicago Cardinals (who now play in Arizona). The Green Bay Packers—the third oldest team—joined the league in 1921.

The New NFL: In 1960, eight football teams banded together and the American Football League was born. The original AFL teams consisted of the Boston Patriots, Buffalo Bills, Dallas Texans, Denver Broncos, Houston Oilers, Los Angeles Chargers, New York Titans, and Oakland Raiders. At the time, the idea of another league seemed ridiculous; in fact, the eight original team owners were nicknamed the "Foolish Club" for their seemingly silly efforts. But the AFL proved to be a rival for the NFL, and the two leagues competed for the best players. This raised the salaries for the players, which was good news for them but bad news for the team owners. The NFL didn't like this. Then the AFL landed its own television contract. The NFL didn't like this either. Then

the AFL considered signing many of the NFL's top quarterbacks. The NFL hated this and decided to end this competition forever: the two leagues merged in 1966. The American Football League became the American Football Conference, one of the two divisions of the NFL; the original NFL teams moved into a division of their own called the National Football Conference. The two conferences held a common draft in 1967 and began competing against one another in the new NFL in 1970.

So, now you know the truth. Football was never born, but it evolved through the years. We are not the first generation of girlfriends to be annoyed with this game and we will not be the last. There was no guy named Earl to blame for football's invention, though we could perhaps point a finger at a loose-headed Viking or give Walter Camp a swift kick in the pants. The game of football has been around for many years and shows no signs of retiring soon. It is time to get with the game, girls. Since you are now committed to becoming a fan, here are a few dates that you should remember:

1875: Budweiser beer makes its debut.

January 27, 1927: Philo T. Farnsworth files his patent for an amazing new invention that will capture pictures from the air. Television is invented.

1928: The most momentous event in the history of relaxation—Edwin Shoemaker and his cousin Edward Knabusch invent an unbelievably comfortable wood-slat porch chair. Numerous names considered for the new chair include "Comfort Carrier," "Sit-N-Snooze," and "Slack-Back." The two Eds choose "La-Z-Boy."

December 28, 1958: Football and TV consummate their marriage when fifty million viewers tune in to the NFL championship game between the Baltimore Colts and the New York Giants at Yankee Stadium. The Colts win 23–17 in sudden-death overtime.

January 26, 1967: Vince Lombardi's Green Bay Packers surprise no one when they beat the Kansas City Chiefs 35–10 in the first Super Bowl.

January 12, 1969: The AFC wins its first Super Bowl in a highly dramatic fashion when Broadway Joe Namath comes through on his guarantee that his underdog team, the New York Jets, would beat the heavily favored Baltimore Colts 16–7.

September 21, 1970: Monday Night Football debuts as the Cleveland Browns beat the New York Jets 31–21. Broadway Joe Namath is far from shining in the nationally televised game and throws three interceptions (passes that were intercepted.)

Year 2000: La-Z-Boy does it again. The days of having to leave the comfort of your recliner to go to the kitchen are over. "Oasis" is the first-ever recliner to feature a beverage cooler built right into the arm of the chair. The refrigeration unit holds up to six cans (twelve ounces each). But that's not all. "Oasis" also features a ten-motor massage and heat system, and a full-size corded telephone with caller ID, making it, without a doubt, the coolest recliner in America!

What the heck is going on?

THE BASIC RULES AND EQUIPMENT

The great coach Vince Lombardi once said, "Football is blocking and tackling. The rest is mythology." Vince is full of crap.

Sure, I agree, it's not easy to follow this game. Sometimes it *is* as complicated as it seems, but sometimes your football guy just likes to make it sound really tricky. But once you learn the basics of the game, it will make sense, even though your football guy probably still won't.

The Game

Every football game is divided into four chunks called quarters. Each quarter is fifteen minutes long. Teams switch ends at the beginning of each quarter. After the first two quarters, there is a halftime break when you will see ceremonies on the field or those silly cheerleaders. This break gives the players a chance to rest and the coach time to instruct the players. Sometimes a tongue-lashing is in order. If the score is tied at the end of the fourth quarter, then a sudden-death overtime is held. The overtime begins just like another quarter. However, the first team to score wins the game. It is very exciting.

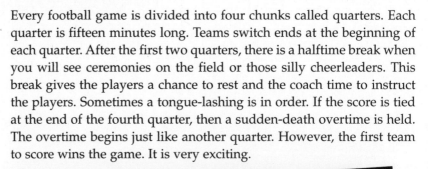

"I have never lost a ball game, but sometimes time has run out on me," said Bobby Layne, quarterback for the Detroit Lions in the 1950s.

GAME TIME

The game clock that keeps track of the playing time does not run constantly through those fifteen-minute quarters. As you may know, a football game doesn't last one hour—it sometimes seems to last as long as a week. The game clock stops for several reasons. They are:

- the end of a quarter
- a time-out is called (each team is allowed three per half)
- a quarterback throws an incomplete pass
- the guy with the ball is out of bounds
- someone is bleeding badly or at least whining about an injury
- a player has been caught being a bad boy by an official and given a penalty
- an official needs to take a measurement (there is a disagreement about the down, or time is needed to spot the ball)
- somebody scores
- the ball has changed possession by a punt or a turnover, or a team has failed to make a first down
- a punt or kick returner catches the ball after a fair catch signal
- when two minutes remain in the quarter

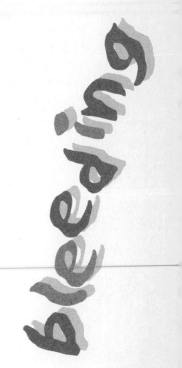

The Stadium

The stadium is the structure that hosts the football game: the field, the stands, our butts, and that beer guy. There are two kinds of stadiums— dome and outdoor. Dome stadiums have closed or retractable roofs to protect fans and players from the elements and their fields are always made of artificial turf. Outdoor stadiums have real grass to play on. Either way, football stadiums generally seat between 60,000 and 150,000 rabid, drunk fans.

THE FIELD

Football is played on a field that is 360 feet long and 160 feet wide. There are two kinds of field surfaces—natural grass and artificial turf. Each surface has pros and cons. Some players don't like turf because it makes their cleats stick, which leads to more injuries. Players also complain of "turf burns" from falling and skidding on the surface. Turf burns are similar to carpet burns. I assume I don't need to explain how you get them.

At each end of this rectangular field are the end zones—the last ten yards at both ends.

Lines: At first, the field lines may look just like your great-uncle's forehead. But unlike your uncle's melon and his story about walking to school uphill both ways, the field lines make sense. The whole field is a grid of white lines that are either painted on the field surface or marked with white chalk. The field may look complicated, but it isn't really.

- The end lines are the lines at the end of the field.
- The sidelines are, you guessed it, at the sides of the field.
- The goal lines are ten yards in from the end lines and mark off the beginning of the end zones.
- The chunk of field marked off by the goal lines and the sidelines is the field of play.
- The solid white, six-foot-wide border around the field is for the officials and the chain crew (the guys with chains who measure if there is some doubt as to whether or not a team has attained enough yards for a first down).
- The line that runs across the very center of the field is the fifty-yard line; it divides the field in half.

When a player is in possession of the ball within these lines, the ball is considered live. When a player goes over these lines, he is considered out of bounds and in big trouble.

Before I forget, I should mention that there are a few more important lines on the field: the yard lines, hash marks, and player benches.

The yard lines run parallel to the goal lines and are at five-yard intervals. They run straight across the field from sideline to sideline. The yard lines enable the officials to measure and mark a team's progression up and down the field. The middle of the field is the fifty-yard line, and the number count moves back from the fifty, on each side (forty-yard line, thirty-five-yard line, etc.), until you reach the goal line, which is the zero-yard line. To better understand the function of the yard lines, see "How to Score" later in this chapter.

Hash marks, which run down the length of the field, resemble two sets of tire tracks created by a very wide truck. They mark off each yard of the field, so there are four hash marks between every yard line. Each hash mark is one foot wide. Altogether there are four sets of hash marks: two run along the sidelines and the other two run down the field seventy feet from the sidelines.

The officials use the hash marks along the sidelines as a guide when a player is either tackled or pushed out of bounds, or when a punt goes out of bounds. In all of these cases, the official returns the ball to the closest hash mark and marks it either on the hash mark or between two of them.

Where are the player benches? They are where those nice shiny butts rest. Behind the six-foot border for the officials is another six-foot area, marked by a broken line, that defines the space for coaches and substitute players only. Six feet behind this area is the bench area. This is where the players watch and rest on benches. Within this space the team doctors and trainers can also look at injured players. The bench area is thirty feet deep and extends to each thirty-two-yard line.

The player bench area is off-limits to fans and media. You are definitely not allowed to hide under the bench and grab butts at will. Fans generally have to stay in the stands; there are selected press-box areas for the media. However, in the player bench area, there is lots of activity. Players often call and talk to coaches located high up in the stadium, and team officials can use phones there to inform the public relations people of team injuries. All this information goes to the press in the press box and out to the television trucks. In turn, the fans read about it in the newspapers or hear about it on TV.

Goalposts: The goalposts sit at the very back of the end zone and look like big slingshots. Kickers try to kick the ball through the posts to score points. If you want to sound cool, you can call this "splitting the uprights." Goalposts are generally painted yellow or white and have a ribbon attached to the top of each post. The ribbons help the officials see the exact top of each post so they can determine if the ball has actually passed between them. The ribbons also indicate the wind conditions so that kickers can make adjustments in their kicks. Originally, the goalposts were located right on the goal line, then they were moved inside the goal line, and finally, in 1974, they were shifted to the very back of the end zone.

Other Junk on the Field: On the sidelines you will see bright orange markers with the yard lines numbered on them. These markers help the players and the fans identify the yard lines. They are made of foam rubber so that a player accidentally colliding with one won't be hurt.

Big orange markers with a "G" on them also help to define the goal lines, and four rubber pylons mark the corners of each end zone.

The Ball

The funny-shaped ball is technically described as a prolate spheroid, and the NFL has very tight rules regarding it. The game ball must be made of a pebble-grained leather in a natural tan color and filled with an inflated rubber bladder. The ball must also have raised white laces to help the players grip and throw it. Each ball must be a Wilson brand and bear the signature of the NFL commissioner, Paul Tagliabue.

It is the home team's responsibility to provide the game balls, thirty-six in an open-air stadium and twenty-four in a dome stadium.

And what happens if you lose the precious ball? I think Chuck has a good ball story for us.

Chuck's Story: Well, you get in big trouble, that's what happens. St. Louis Cardinal receiver Dave Steif was so excited when he caught a touchdown pass in 1978 against the Detroit Lions that he chucked the ball into the broadcasters' booth. The officials didn't think it was funny and fined him.

The Equipment

Watching a football game can sometimes be terrifying. If you are like me, watching those guys get squashed is a scary sight. I always wonder how players can take such hits and still be able to move afterward. Well, girls, all that equipment does help, so let's just see what they are packing under those wonderfully tight little outfits.

HELMETS AND FACE MASKS

I like football helmets; in fact, I wish every sport used them. Football helmets not only have a chin strap to keep them secure, but they also have air-filled pockets inside to help prevent concussions. The air in the pockets can be adjusted to make sure the helmet fits tightly and will not move when a player gets hit.

All football helmets have a face mask. The mask is made of a round, metal, cage-type guard. The amount of coverage of this mask depends on the player's position. A lineman's mask has a lot of bars to protect his face from opposition players. The quarterbacks and receivers wear a much more open mask so they can see clearly. Believe it or not, it wasn't until January 1962 that it became illegal to grab a player's face mask.

PADS

Football players wear pads to help absorb the terrible impact from hitting and being hit. They must balance the amount of padding necessary for protection and mobility.

The shoulder pads are the most important pads, as they protect the shoulders, the chest, and the ribs. Some shoulder pads also protect the upper part of the arms.

Players also wear thigh, elbow, hip, and knee pads to protect themselves.

THE JERSEY

The jersey is a tight-fitting shirt that helps keep the shoulder pads in place. It also identifies each player—which team he is on, his player number, and his name. In the NFL, players in certain positions wear certain numbers; this system was adopted in 1973.

- Kickers and quarterbacks wear 1 to 19.
- Defensive backs and running backs wear 20 to 49.
- Linebackers and centers wear 50 to 59.
- Offensive linemen (guards and tackles) and defensive ends wear 60 to 79.
- Receivers (tight ends and wide receivers) wear 80 to 89.

Sometimes centers wear numbers up to 79 and defensive linemen and linebackers wear 90 to 99.

This numbering system is really helpful because you can always identify who is on the field and what position they play. If you are really cool, you may even be able to read what kind of play the coach has in mind.

Usually, the visiting team wears white and the home team wears colored uniforms.

THE PANTS

Ahhhh, the pants. On behalf of all the women in the world, I would like to thank the NFL for the pants. We all know why we should, and do, enjoy football. It has something to do with those wonderful, tight, shiny buns bouncing across the field like spring fawns.

Football pants have always been tight, for player comfort and speed. It is also important that defenders have nothing to catch hold of (though, given the opportunity, I could probably get a big handful of something).

SHOES AND CLEATS

Proper shoes are always important, but when you risk tearing apart your knees and ruining your million-dollar career, footwear becomes even more important. A football player's style of shoe depends on the field surface that he is playing on—artificial or grass—and on the field conditions. When the conditions change during the course of a game, players often switch shoes.

For artificial surfaces, football players prefer a basketball type of shoe that has small nubby cleats on the bottom. Artificial turf can be sticky, so players want to glide over it rather than stop quickly, which can cause trauma to their bodies. On slippery natural grass, the players prefer a deeper cleat for more traction. Because traction is of utmost importance, a player will often carry many types of shoes to adapt to the playing surface.

Football players are big boys and they have big feet (and we all know what that means, nudge, nudge, wink, wink). One of the largest pairs of football shoes belonged to Cincinnati's Willie Anderson. Willie wore a whopping size-nineteen shoe.

UNIFORM RULES

The NFL is pretty strict on their uniform rules; they like to keep the boys looking sharp. Players are not allowed to wear torn uniforms like you see in high school or college play when the player has cut the jersey to expose his handsome, rock-hard, six-pack belly. In NFL play, all jerseys must remain tucked inside the players' pants. The NFL also has rules on shield and logo placement. They even regulate the tape used on the players' shoes, pants, and socks.

In 1980, Reggie Williams of the Cincinnati Bengals learned how important the uniform regulations were to the NFL. Poor Reggie was fined $1,000. And what sin did he commit? Reggie's socks slipped down to his ankles during a play against the Houston Oilers. One thousand dollars for droopy socks. It's a good thing the NFL hasn't seen my Aunt Nellie's saggy knees—she'd owe them her life savings.

Teena:
Hey Chuck, how does the NFL feel about panty hose?

Chucky says:
Awww, this story is kind of creepy, but okay. Apparently the NFL likes panty hose. On one very cold day in Shea Stadium, the New York Jets came up with the idea to wear panty hose to help keep warm. Needless to say, some of the players were not thrilled with the cross-dressing idea, but they gave it a try. And the panty hose worked. As the Jets' equipment manager at the time said, "The panty hose are just great. They keep our guys warm and they are not as bulky as thermal underwear."

Teena:
I bet it also made them feel smooth and sexy.

Panty Hose

Getting the Game Started

Now that you understand the field and the equipment, it's time to figure out what the heck they are doing out there. We will start from the beginning.

THE COIN TOSS

A football game starts with a coin toss. Three captains from each team meet at the center of the field with the referee. The ref has the coin, and one captain on the visiting team calls the toss. If the visiting team wins the toss, they have to make a decision: Do they want to receive the kick or kick to the home team?

Usually the winner of the coin toss has the ball kicked to them. This way, they can immediately gain possession of the ball and try to score points. But if the wind is blowing in such a way as to make throwing and kicking difficult, the coin toss winner may decide to kick off to the opposition. This gives the opposition a chance to score, but the coin toss winner will have the wind working with them during the crucial final quarter, when scoring is really important. And how does the kickoff work, you ask?

THE KICKOFF

A kickoff puts the ball into play at the start of the first and third quarters and after every touchdown and field goal. The team receiving the ball lines up on the line of scrimmage. The kicking team's placekicker puts the ball on a tee at his own thirty-yard line. He kicks the ball to the receiving team. The player or players on the receiving team assigned to return the ball (conveniently called the returners) catch it and make a beeline toward the opposition's goal line, or the returner will down the ball in the end zone for a touchback.

HOW TO GET DOWN

The whole point of football is to make your way down the field toward the opposition's goal line and score. The fashion in which the players move down the field is called downs. You go down the field by getting downs; it makes sense. The word "down" can essentially be changed into the word "chance." The offense has four chances, or four downs, to advance the ball ten yards down the field. If the offensive team gets ten yards in four downs or fewer, then they get another set of four downs to get ten yards closer to the end zone. The only tricky part to remember is that each chance is called a down, and when a team successfully completes their set of four chances, they are said to have made a first down. If the offense keeps making their downs, then they can keep on truckin' down the field in their attempt to score. If, on the other hand, the offensive team knows that they will not make their ten yards in four downs, they often decide to punt the ball to the defenders on the fourth and last down. Punting means that the offense will kick the ball (without a tee this time) as deep into the opposition's zone as possible so that the receiving team has a longer distance to travel before they can score. Once the ball has been received by the defenders, then the first set of downs begins for them. Now they try to make their way down the field for a scoring opportunity.

During the game, the announcers yack constantly. They throw out numbers that don't seem to make any sense. What they are actually describing is the offensive team's progress. For example, when the announcers say, "First and ten," they mean that the offense is ready to take their first chance and needs to advance ten yards to complete the first down. When the announcers say, "Second and eight," they mean that the offensive team advanced two yards on their previous down. Now the team is beginning their second chance and needs to go eight more yards to complete their first down. It is quite simple: the announcers tell us what down (or chance) it is, and how far the offense must go in order to achieve first down and earn another chance to move down the field.

How To Score

We now know that teams use a series of downs to move down the field, but how do they actually get points? There are a number of ways to score in football: touchdowns, extra points, two-point conversions, field goals, and safeties.

Touchdowns: Touchdowns create the greatest excitement because they are worth six points—the most points possible in football. A touchdown is awarded when an offensive player carries the ball and crosses the plane of the opposing team's goal line. This means that if the player with the ball crosses the goal line in midair, and then is tackled and knocked back over the line, the touchdown still counts. As long as the ball crosses the plane at some point, however brief, then a touchdown is awarded.

Extra Point and Two-Point Conversion: The extra point is also known as the point after a touchdown (or PAT, if you want to sound cool). After a touchdown, another down is awarded to the scoring team to attempt a PAT. To get this extra point, the kicker must kick the ball between the uprights of the goalpost and above the crossbar. This down begins at the two-yard line.

The two-point conversion occurs when the offensive team carries the ball over the goal line or passes it into the end zone, like a touchdown, instead of kicking it through the uprights. Again, the team starts this two-point conversion attempt at the two-yard line.

Field Goals: Field goals are attempted when a team is going for a touchdown but gets slowed down at the opposition's thirty-yard line. It's a consolation prize for a good attempt. A field goal attempt is successful when a kicker boots the ball (which is held by a teammate) through the uprights. In this case, the ball cannot touch the ground or any of the kicker's teammates en route. If the field goal is missed, the team doesn't score and loses the ball. If the field goal attempt was from inside the twenty-yard line, the defense gets the ball at the twenty-yard line. If the attempt was outside the twenty, then the defense takes possession from the spot of the kick.

Safeties: I find the scoring of safeties quite confusing, so follow me closely. A safety is worth two points. The important thing to remember about safeties is the word "impetus." Impetus is the action of the offensive player who gives the ball motion; it's a fancy word for the ball movement by an offensive guy. For a safety to be scored, the offensive ballcarrier must provide the impetus; he cannot be pushed around by the defense. So far so good?

Okay. This is a safety: when a team forces the opposition to down the ball in their own end zone, they get two points (a safety). What the hell is a downed ball? Well, the ball is "down" if the quarterback, running back, or receiver is tackled or if they go out of bounds. It's easy—bring the ball into your own end zone and let it go down. It's a safety for the other team.

There are still other ways to be awarded a safety (the kicking team screwing up in the end zone or a blocked punt going out of bounds), but by now your head is probably splitting like mine. So my advice is this: if you don't know why your team just got two points, assume it was a safety (listen to the play-by-play guy, he'll tell you). If your football guy asks you anything about it, tell him that you think the living room should be redecorated; that'll shut him up.

Basic Strategy

So, we now know how the players move around the field and score, but what is the game plan? There are a million strategies and formations that coaches have cooked up since the beginning of football. We don't really need to learn them. Just think of football as a giant game of chess—full-contact chess with really, really big pieces that can attack and crush the other really, really big pieces.

To move the ball up the field in football, you can either run with the ball or pass it to other players. It is safer to run with the ball (less chance of a turnover) than to pass it. A strong running game gives a team the option to pass instead of being pressured to pass. Passes may be completed, incomplete, or intercepted. A pass is incomplete if the ball is not caught, is caught and then dropped, or is caught out of bounds. The ball is then ruled dead and returned to the line of scrimmage. A pass is intercepted if the defense gains possession of the ball while it is in the air. This is also called a turnover. On average, only one out of three passes is completed, which is why running is often preferred. But it is also important to remember that a completed pass usually gains more yardage than a run.

Tips on Watching
the Game

Football can be confusing, but it is also a stop-and-go game. If you watch football on television, it is almost impossible to miss the plays, unless you are out of the room or unconscious. Many cameras capture the action on the field and you can watch the replays from many angles, many times. This allows you to figure out what just happened while you enjoy those agile bods tumbling in slow motion.

Don't forget to keep your eye on the corner of the television screen. The graphic there will tell you what down it is, how much yardage the offense needs to gain to make first down, how much time is left, and the score.

Watch the line of scrimmage. The number of players on the line and the positions they take will alert you to the upcoming play. Here are some specific things to look out for:

- If the defenders seem to be creeping up to the line of scrimmage, they plan to either blitz the quarterback or rush into the running lanes to block a running play.
- If only three defensive linemen are lined up close to the line of scrimmage, the defense expects the offense to pass.
- If more than four defensive backs are on the field, the defense is preparing to prevent a pass completion.
- If the offense has four receivers on the field, the quarterback will probably be throwing the ball.

Don't worry too much about the announcers' jargon. With their weird words and loads of statistics, they can be quite confusing. As you watch more games (and finish reading this informative and entertaining book), you will begin to understand them—and even appreciate them if you need a potty break.

Who's got the ball?

I know what you mean; a bunch of big guys running around bumping into each other, a whistle blows, and the team advances an eighth of an inch down the field. One moment, the players on the field are Greek gods, then the next moment, they are big, fat 500-pounders bumping their blubbery bods around. Believe it or not, there is rhyme or reason for the variety in the size of the players. And believe it or not, those guys actually have a plan and are not just maniacs trying to crush each other. This chapter will explain each player's position and why some players have buns of steel and others have buns of cheeseburgers.

The Team

Each football team is essentially three teams in one: the offense, the defense, and the special teams. Keeping everyone straight can sometimes be difficult. So, girlfriend, we will look at each part of the team and talk about their job (and their butts). But first we have to get a few things straight. If the team is trying to score, their offensive line is on the field. If the team is trying to keep the other team from scoring, their defensive line is on the field. And if there is a special kicking situation coming up (field goal, conversion attempt, punt), the special team is on the field. But no matter what part of the team is playing—offense, defense, or special team—there are only eleven players on the field per side.

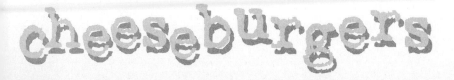

cheeseburgers

The Offensive Boys

The offensive team's job is to gain yardage and get into the defender's end zone to score points. This is accomplished in one of three ways: by running the ball, by passing the ball, or by kicking the ball. The coach decides the play, the quarterback calls it, and then everyone else moves into place. There are a zillion plays in football. I could spend hours explaining them to you, but they really aren't that interesting. So let's just say that the plays are designed to make space and time for the quarterback to throw, hand off, or run the ball. Offensive plays involve blocking, handling the ball, running, and receiving. There, that wasn't so bad, was it?

Eleven offensive players are on the field at any one time. There are only seven offensive positions, so depending on the formation that has been chosen, the number of players in each position varies.

It's like getting dressed to seduce your guy. If you are trying to distract your football guy from the game, you'd better put on the full "I'm gonna rock your world" gear. Let's say you normally wear eleven things: a bustier, a garter, two stockings, a G-string, two bracelets, two earrings, and a pair of stilettos. But last week your guy bought you two beautiful new bracelets that match the ones you normally wear. You know that wearing them will drive him wild so you decide to ditch the two earrings tonight and wear four bracelets instead. You can mix and match within your seduction outfit in the same way that the offensive line changes its formation.

An average offensive line consists of:

- a quarterback
- a center
- two guards
- two tackles
- two wide receivers
- a tight end
- two running backs

THE QUARTERBACK: WHAT A STUD

Mike Tomczak, a Chicago Bears quarterback, once told of a conversation he had with David Fulcher, a Cincinnati Bengals safety: "He said something about how he was coming after me, about how he was going to knock me out of the game—you know, the usual NFL-type camaraderie."

Yes, the quarterback (also known as the QB) has a tough job. He is the most important player on the team and that is why he is also the highest paid. He is the leader of the pack. His job is to guide the offensive team and lead them toward the end zone, and score points. He does this by receiving the plays from the coach via a hearing device in his helmet. Wouldn't it be great if we could have one of these little gadgets placed on our guy's head? We could send a message like this: "Don't forget to get milk on the way home. Hey, my birthday is coming up; don't get me any more bracelets."

The quarterback receives plays from the coach, but, when necessary, he must also change the plays that the coach has called. If, at the line of scrimmage, the quarterback feels that the play will not work or that the defense has figured out what they are up to, he will change the play by calling an "audible." That is the "Blah, blah, blah" that you hear before the "Hut, hut, hut." The players on the offensive team know these codes and what they mean. The codes tell them what the play is and how it will change.

Above all, a quarterback must be a born leader who can make good decisions under enormous pressure. He must have good arm strength and a quick ball release. He must be fast and lean. He must be very competitive and intelligent. It also appears that quarterbacks must have perfectly straight teeth. If only he also cleaned, cooked, and shopped, this guy would be perfect.

CENTER, GUARDS, AND TACKLES: A CENTER SANDWICH

The interior line is the group name for the players in the middle of the offensive line: the center, two guards, and two tackles. It's like your guy; he is part of a larger group called "the men who sit on your couch drinking beer all Sunday afternoon," which is a subgroup of "men in general." The group called "the men who sit on your couch drinking beer all Sunday afternoon" consists of your guy, his buddy Darrell, and his other buddy Darrell. The interior line is a subgroup of the offensive line.

The center is the middle guy, positioned at the center of the interior line. The left guard and right guard are on each side of the center. On each side of the guards are the left and right tackles. You might find it helpful to imagine a "center sandwich" with "guard/tackle bread." Mmmmm, delicious!

The Center: The center is positioned in the center of the line of scrimmage. He has the most demanding position on the offensive line. The center must deliver the ball on the snap to the quarterback; therefore, he must know the signal count by the quarterback (the "Hut, hut, hut"). He must also direct the blocking of the rest of the line. In many ways, he acts as a coach on the field. He directs his team according to the alignment of the defensive players. He does this by using coded words that the defenders don't understand.

Centers need to be fast, smart, levelheaded, and brave. They need to be tough enough to receive hits by the defenders and focused enough to hold their concentration when directing their teammates.

The Guards: The guards are positioned on either side of the center. They are some of the best blockers in the game. Their job is to help "guard" the quarterback (thus their name). They use their arms, hands, and shoulders to move defenders out of the way and give the quarterback time to execute the play. The left and right guards can be huge, hulking players or small, quick guys, depending on the style of the offense.

The Tackles: The tackles are positioned on the outer-left and outer-right side of the guards. Tackles are generally the biggest of the interior linemen and the most athletic. Their job at the end of the line is tough. They need to block some of the game's best defensive linemen to help the quarterback. Their name can be confusing because tackles aren't actually allowed to tackle. They only block for the player who has the ball. They need to be very agile and strong.

These five players on the interior line (the center, the two guards, and the two tackles) play together as a blocking unit in what is called the "pits" or the "trenches." They do not receive passes.

THE WIDE RECEIVERS AND TIGHT END: GIVE US THE DAMN BALL

"Receivers" is the group name for the players who receive passes. Receivers consist of the wide receivers and tight end.

The Wide Receivers: The wide receivers are positioned on the outside ends of the line of scrimmage. Wide receivers can be tall or short, but they must be fast and lean with nimble hands. They must be able to concentrate under pressure, and they must be physically strong to take punishment from the defenders. The wide receiver's job is to run down the field, catch the ball when the quarterback throws it to him, and keep running until he is either squished or gets a touchdown. The wide receivers are often referred to by other names, depending on the role they play and where they line up. Sometimes they are referred to as a split end or flanker. It's like your football guy. His mother may have named him Stephen, but sometimes you call him Stevie-Stud-Muffin, Zorro, Tarzan, or Big-Beer-Guzzling-Lump-on-the-Couch.

> Chuck:
> Hey, did you know that a former NFL linebacker actually played Tarzan in the 1960s? It was Mike Henry.

The Tight End: The tight end is usually positioned at the end of the line of scrimmage, between the tackle and the wide receiver. Because he does more heavy-duty blocking, the tight end doesn't need to be as fast as wide receivers. The tight end is expected to be a good blocker as well as an excellent pass receiver.

THE RUNNING BACKS: FAST AS A SPEEDING BULLET

Running backs are positioned in the backfield, behind the quarterback. They are the players who primarily, surprise, run the ball. Running backs are also allowed to catch the ball. Running backs must be able to take the punishing physical contact they receive on every play. They come in all shapes and sizes, and can run like hell. Like your Stud-Muffin or Couch-Lump, running backs also have different names depending on their job. They are sometimes called halfback or fullback.

Let's take a look at the basic offensive formation:

QB: quarterback   T: tackle   TE: tight end
C: center   WR: wide receiver   RB: running back
G: guard

seduction

You are now familiar with the basic offensive formation. And like the different formations of your seduction outfit, which varies according to your style and plan for seduction, offensive formations can change, too. Maybe the coach feels that two tight ends would produce better results; for that matter, maybe you do, too.

The Great Defenders

Put simply, the defensive team's job is to react to the play of the offense, and prevent them from gaining yardage and scoring points.

How can the defensive team predict what the offense's plan is without being psychic? First of all, the defense watches films of the opposition to help them figure out the team's strengths and weaknesses. How the offensive line lines up also gives them hints on whether it will be a run, pass, or kick. These factors, as well as body language, eye contact, head movement, and the conversations between the opposition, give the defense an idea of the offense's strategy.

The defense calls its lineup structure the "alignment" (as opposed to the offense's "formation"). There are many defensive alignments, and just like offensive formations, they are not that interesting to discuss. Let's just say that there are eleven players on the defensive team and five different positions. The coach chooses how many players of each position according to his great game plan.

An average defensive alignment consists of the following players:

- two defensive tackles
- two defensive ends
- three linebackers
- two cornerbacks
- two safeties

DEFENSIVE TACKLES AND DEFENSIVE ENDS: THE BIG BOYS

Defensive linemen are the players in the middle of the line of scrimmage, consisting of the tackles and the ends. Defensive linemen must combine speed and size (on the defensive team, they are the heaviest at about 300 pounds) with enough strength to endure the thousand or so hits they receive in a season. They also must be tall enough to see above and around the offensive linemen, with strong instincts in reading the offensive stance. Their main job is to stop the run at the line of scrimmage and to rush (chase down) the quarterback if a passing play develops. They try to make tackles and record sacks (tackle the quarterback while he's attempting to pass). These tackles and sacks are added to each lineman's personal statistics, and are so valuable that if two players sack the quarterback or tackle a player, each will be credited with half a sack or an assist for the tackle.

Remember, when the divine defensive plan from the coach changes, the player positions also change. Defensive plans are like offensive plans—and our seduction plans; they change according to what will get the job done.

The Defensive Tackles: The defensive tackles line up in the center of the line of scrimmage. Their job is to get through the blockers on the offensive team and squash the player with the ball. On running plays, they target the running backs, and on passing plays, they go for the quarterback. Like the offensive linemen and your football guy, the tackles go by different names depending on their role and position on the field. They are also referred to as the nose tackle or the under tackle.

The Defensive Ends: The two defensive linemen who line up on either side of the defensive tackles are the defensive ends. Their job varies depending on those boring and confusing defensive plays. Generally, the ends are responsible for chasing the quarterback out of the pocket (the space the offensive players have made for him to run or pass in) and sacking his sorry butt, or they go after the running backs. These guys are smaller than the defensive tackles, but they still weigh in at about 290 pounds. Not too small in my books. Depending on where they line up, the ends are sometimes called the open ends, the elephant ends (or, as I like to call them, the elephant butts), and the pass-rushing ends.

THE LINEBACKERS: THE REALLY BIG BOYS

Linebackers come in all shapes and sizes because they play many roles on the field. They may weigh 215 pounds or 270 pounds; they may be fast and lean enough to go after the running backs or strong and big enough to clog up the middle to stifle the offense's plans. Their main jobs are to tackle the guy with the ball and cover the receivers. All linebackers need to be smart, have strong instincts, and be able to react immediately to the snap of the ball. Like quarterbacks, they make calls and direct the rest of the team. Linebackers sometimes leave their assigned positions to blitz (which is football speak for pulverize) the quarterback. They are heavily responsible for putting pressure on the quarterback. Depending on where they line up, linebackers are sometimes called Sam linebacker (do you get the feeling that they ran out of names and just made it up on the spur of the moment?), Willy linebacker (Willy linebackers are usually smaller and faster than the other linebackers; hence they are called Willy after all those small, quick Willys in the world), and Mike linebacker.

The linebackers are aligned in various ways with various jobs depending on the coach's defensive strategy (which we don't care to know about because they are really, really boring.) Generally, they can be found in the middle of the alignment, behind the defensive ends and tackles.

THE CORNERBACKS AND SAFETIES: ONE MORE CHANCE TO DIE

The defensive backs (which make up the "secondary") are situated in the backfield of the defense. These are the guys in the back row, the team's last hope to stop the offensive players. Depending on the defensive scheme, the secondary can consist of three, four, five, six, or seven defensive backs, but usually only two cornerbacks and two safeties are used.

When another defensive back is added to the usual four, this configuration is called a "nickel back." When two defensive backs are added to the regular four, it is called a "dime back" (two nickel backs added together to equal a dime back). Who makes up this crap?

The Cornerbacks: Cornerbacks line up against the receivers (tight ends and wide receivers) and are in charge of squashing them. The cornerback is the fastest of all the defensive backs. He usually weighs between 180 and 190 pounds, is at least six feet tall, and is able to do a forty-yard dash in 4.4 seconds. The defense usually uses two cornerbacks. The cornerback's job is one that does not brook excuses. If he messes up, the offensive player will get by and score points.

The Safeties: The safeties are positioned in the very back of the defensive alignment. The safeties are like the quarterbacks of the secondary. From their vantage point, they can instruct the rest of the secondary to make coverage changes according to the opposition's formation. The middle

linebacker focuses his attention on the defensive linemen and is generally too far away to yell to the secondary. The safeties coordinate the secondary's coverages and consult the linebackers for assistance. They use secret hand signals to do this. Safeties are good tacklers and agile runners, so they can retreat quickly in order to make coverage changes (called dropping into pass coverage). Depending on their alignment, safeties are also called strong safeties or free safeties.

This is what the defensive alignment looks like:

T: tackle   C: cornerback
DE: defensive end   S: safety
LB: linebacker

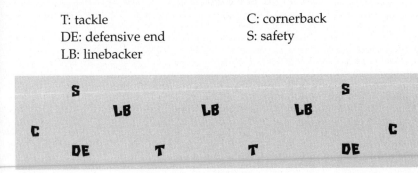

It is all rather simple, isn't it? Isn't it? It is all about making sure the offensive team gets crushed. Crush them!

Special Teams

Walt Michaels, the New York Jets coach, once said, "A man who has no fear belongs in a mental institution... or on special teams." All football players are special and we love them the same, but some players are especially special and they are on the special team. These guys have very specialized assignments and skills specific to the kicking game. The players on the special team usually also play positions on either the defensive line or the offensive line. Coaches say that special teams play about one-third of the football game. They are called in for the most intense parts of the game, and their impact on the outcome can make or break a game. The players on this eleven-man unit are willing to challenge themselves and test their skills. They need to be courageous and able to think clearly under pressure. When the special team is on the field, anything can happen and the play is fast, furious, and all over the field. To understand special teams, we must first understand the difference between placekicking and punting.

Placekicking occurs when the ball is held in place, a la Charlie Brown and Lucy, or when it is placed on a tee and then kicked. Placekicking is used for field goals and the point after touchdowns. Punting is when the ball is snapped back to the punter, who then kicks the ball from above the ground. The team will decide to punt when they are in a fourth-down situation with no hope of reaching their ten yards. Good hang time (the time that passes as the ball is in the air) is important for both type of kicks. A long hang time allows the rest of the kicker's team to get downfield and in position to squish the player who catches the kick.

FIELD GOALS AND PATS

THE OFFENSE

If the offense scores a touchdown, they will attempt a point after touchdown with the special team. These same players will be called on the field if the offense is close to the end zone but knows that it will not make it by their fourth down. The special team will then attempt a field goal. This special team consists of:

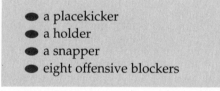

- a placekicker
- a holder
- a snapper
- eight offensive blockers

The Placekickers: The placekicker is generally the smallest player on the team. His job is to kick the ball long, accurately, and hard. The place-kicker lines up behind and slightly to the side of the holder.

The Holder: The holder catches the ball from the snapper, then quickly spots it on the ground for the kicker to kick. The holder is usually the backup quarterback or the punter. He lines up directly behind the snapper.

The Snapper: The snapper passes the ball back between his legs to the holder. The snapper lines up in the middle of the line of scrimmage. He is usually the center from the offensive line.

The Offensive Blockers: The offensive blockers' job is to block the defense so the kicker can kick the ball. These players are usually offensive or defensive linemen. They line up along the line of scrimmage, four on each side of the snapper.

THE DEFENSE

When the offense is planning a field goal or PAT, the defense puts their own special team on the field. The defense's job is to try and block the kick. They must also watch for fake kicks, where the other team tries to run or pass for a first down or touchdown. The defensive special team consists of:

- ten defensive rushers
- one defensive safety

The Defensive Rushers: The defensive rushers' job is to block the kick. Some defensive rushers will try and push through the blockers to get to the ball before it is kicked. Some rushers will use their height and jumping talents to try and get a big hand on the ball as it goes by them. These players can come from almost any position on the team, as long as they are tall and fearless. All ten of the defensive rushers line up on the line of scrimmage.

The Defensive Safety: This guy is the lookout. Once in a while, the offense will fake a kick. Instead, they will run or pass from this kicking formation. The defense will usually keep one or two players back, just in case this happens. These players are usually defensive backs, and they line up behind the rushers.

PUNTING

THE OFFENSE

If the offense realizes that it is not going to be able to complete their ten yards by the fourth down, they will decide to punt the ball to the other team. The special team that is called out for this special job consists of:

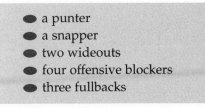

- a punter
- a snapper
- two wideouts
- four offensive blockers
- three fullbacks

The Punter: The punter's job is to kick the ball far and straight, with the average punt traveling forty yards. The punter's job is so important that he doesn't play any other position on the team. He lines up in the backfield, behind the rest of the team.

The Snapper: The snapper passes the ball back between his legs to the punter. He lines up in the middle of the line of scrimmage. He is usually the center from the offensive line.

The Wideouts: The wideouts have the fun job of going downfield and trying to squash the punt returner. They are really fast and really tough. They can come from any position on the team. They line up on each end of the line of scrimmage.

The Offensive Blockers: The offensive blockers must block the defense so that the punter can kick the ball. They are usually offensive or defensive linemen. Two line up on each side of the snapper.

The Fullback: The fullback acts as the last line of defense. He stops the other team's players from wrecking the punt. The fullback also signals the snapper to hike the ball back to the punter. Fullbacks are usually linebackers, running backs, or offensive linemen. They line up behind the offensive blockers and in front of and off to the side of the punter.

THE DEFENSE

The offense has to punt the ball to someone—these are the guys who receive the punt. As the offense tries to punt the ball, the defense tries to block it so that they gain possession closer to the end zone. The team that does this consists of:

- a punt returner
- two return blockers
- eight defensive rushers

The Punt Returner: First of all, punt returners are completely insane. Their job is to catch the punt and run toward the opposing team's end zone. If they don't want to run the ball, they can signal for a fair catch. This means that once they catch the ball, they cannot move, nor can the opposing team hit them. The play will begin again where the ball was caught. Punt returners are the fastest guys on the team (usually wide receivers or defensive backs). They line up in the backfield.

The Return Blockers: Return blockers run ahead of the punt returner and try to defend him against the wideouts. The longer they can delay the returner from being tackled, the farther downfield he will get. These guys can come from any position on the team. They line up on either side of the punt returner.

The Defensive Rushers: The defensive rushers do the same job here as they did on field goals—they try and block the ball by jumping up and batting it with their hands.

The special team's job is to drastically improve their field position or to score. They are under a lot of pressure and rarely receive the recognition that they deserve. No wonder that special team players are often the strangest of the bunch. They are usually the most eccentric of the players. Take Travis Jervey, of the Green Bay Packers, for example. Travis has a pet lion. If you like wild men, hook up with a special team player. They are the craziest of all.

Now you know that football is not just a bunch of big guys running around like really mean chickens with their heads cut off. There is a reason for their running. You also understand why some players look like jumbo jigglers and others look like rock-hard hotties, and why some guys need to be able to run like a lean cheetah and some guys need to be like a big, old elephant's butt, squashing their opponents. It all makes sense now, doesn't it, sisters? Whether your favorite player is a cool cat or an elephant's behind, he does have a specific job to do. Now, if only you could understand why your Elephant Ass won't get off the couch and do his job!

ECCENTRIC

Who's the boss?

MAYHEM

OFFICIALS, COACHES, OWNERS, AND THE NFL

Football is not the disorganized mayhem and chaos that it appears to be. It is actually well-orchestrated mayhem and chaos, and the bandleaders are the officials, coaches, owners, and the all-seeing NFL organization. These are the people and the organization who enforce the rules, direct the players, pay the salaries, and basically run the show.

NFL Officials: The Game Gods

Of necessity, football officials place themselves at the center of a storm—in the middle of twenty-two huge padded men on a field. Just off the field are more huge padded men along with their wild-eyed, foul-mouthed coaches. In football, there are no separated bench areas like there are in hockey, and there are no quaint little "dugouts" as in baseball. Football players can reach out and touch, slap, and choke the men in stripes. Beyond the sidelines and surrounding the field on all sides are about 70,000 totally psychotic, die-hard, face-painted, costume-wearing fans, many of whom would rather stick ferrets down their pants than watch their team lose because some idiot ref missed a call. Beyond those live fans are the millions of couch quarterbacks watching at home or in sports bars who wonder if any judge in their home city would actually find them guilty if they caused bodily harm to the ref. And these referees, umpires, linesmen, and other zebras are only part-time employees who carry nothing to use in their own self-defense but a whistle and a yellow flag to signal penalties. They do it because they love football. Or maybe they're masochists and just love being told every week that they're stupid, blind, ignorant, feeble, idiotic, slow, dim-witted, obtuse, and wrong about everything they do and say.

And here they are… your officials and what they do that makes them such jerk-faced morons.

THE REFEREE

The boss. Zebra. Blindy. Mr. Coke Bottle Glasses. Goofball. Turd. The referee is the main official who oversees the game's flow by starting the clock and placing the ball in play. He has the final authority on scoring and the number of downs if there is any disagreement. After the ball is snapped, the referee mainly keeps his eye on the quarterback. He is watching for any illegal hits on the QB or any illegal blocks around him.

During kicking situations, the referee watches the hoofer and for any illegal contact with the game's daintiest performers. The referee also gets the cool job of using his microphone to announce all penalties and the end of each quarter. Despite being the bad guy for both teams, the referee is the only zebra who wears a good-guy-style white hat.

THE UMPIRE

No, he doesn't call balls and strikes, but your wise-ass thoughts show you're at least thinking sports. That's a good sign that you're well on your way to becoming a dumb jock. Congrats. In football, the umpire gets to play fashion and manners critic. His main job is to watch the line of scrimmage during the play. He gets to rule on players' equipment, as well as on their conduct and actions on the scrimmage line, as in, "Darryl, you know it's illegal to hold Leon by the nostrils. And you know something, purple makes you look fat; I'd change teams if I were you." The umpire rules on the legality of the contact between the players at the line of scrimmage, and he calls most of the holding violations. The umpire also records all time-outs, the winner of the coin toss, and all scores. If it is raining on game day, the umpire has a very special duty: he wipes the ball when it's wet.

THE HEAD LINESMAN

The head linesman's job is mostly done before the snap, as he watches for offsides, encroachments, and a few other scrimmage line infractions.

The linesman is also the man who rules on whether the ball (or the pass receiver) goes out of bounds.

He also helps the referee keep track of the downs and keeps his chain crew moving down the field, marking field position, downs, and yards to go. The linesman does all of this for you so that you can follow the play more easily. On running plays, the linesman determines how far the ball was carried and signals this to the ref or umpire.

THE LINE JUDGE

This guy gets to do some straddling. Unfortunately, it's nothing too exciting. He straddles the line of scrimmage on the side of the field opposite the linesman. He's also a clock-watcher who acts as a backup for the clock operator. Like the linesman, he's responsible for calling offsides, encroachments, and other scrimmage line stuff before the snap. He assists the umpire with holding calls and watches for illegal use of the hands at the end of the line of scrimmage. He assists the referee with false start calls. Generally, the line judge is a very helpful guy.

The line judge also has the key responsibility of telling the ref when each period is over, just in case he misses the firing of the signal gun, the entrance of the cheerleaders, the mass exodus of players for the Gatorade jugs, or the long stretch of beer commercials.

THE BACK JUDGE

My job during the huddle; Chuck's job during the halftime show; and some stripe-wearing clown's job while the football game is on. Yes, I'm talking about being a back judge.

The back judge lines up in the defensive zone on the same side of the field as the line judge. He rules on holding, or illegal use of the hands by the receivers or by defenders working against the receivers. The back judge rules on whether receivers or runners are out of bounds on his sideline. Together with the field judge, the back judge makes that tough judgment call on whether a field goal attempt has made it through the uprights.

THE FIELD JUDGE

The field judge is positioned back, way back, twenty-five yards down-field on the tight end's side. Like me, he watches the tight end… and makes sure the player is blocking legally or that no one around him is breaking any rules.

The field judge also times the intermission between the two quarters of each half and keeps time on the 40/25-second clock. The 40/25-second clock is used for two things: (1) when a play ends, the team with the ball has forty seconds to begin another play or they are punished with a delay of game penalty, or (2) if the game is stopped because of a change of possession, a time-out, an injury, a measurement, or any other unusual delay of the game, a twenty-five-second interval exists between plays. The field judge can also decide on catching, recovery, or illegal touching of a loose ball beyond the line of scrimmage. He can call pass interferences, fair catch infractions, and clippings on kick returns. He joins his buddy the back judge to rule whether or not field goals and conversions are successful.

THE SIDE JUDGE

The side judge basically does the same thing as the back judge, except on the opposite side of the field. He doesn't get to call field goals, though, and on field goal attempts he becomes a second umpire.

CRIME AND PUNISHMENT

Mike "The Animal" Curtis, linebacker for the Baltimore Colts in the 1960s and 1970s, once said, "I like football because I can do things in it that I'd be arrested for on the streets."

It's hard to believe, I know, and I used to think the only rule in football was to make sure a guy stayed down when you knocked him down, or you'd be in big trouble. I figured with all that padding they must be able to smash each other upside the head, in the kidneys, even in the groin, and feel no pain. If it is legal for players to drive their helmets into the guts of their opponents and crumple the ball-carriers up like little papier-mâché men, what is considered unlawful?

Well, actually there are a few things you just can't do in football. You can't haul a guy down by the face mask. You can't knock the skinny little kicker on his butt while he's standing there with one leg high in the air admiring his fine, spiraling rocket launch. You can't punch, kick, or spit on an opponent or an official. And, while it isn't in the official rule book, it is considered bad football etiquette to rinse your dirty jockstrap in the Gatorade bucket.

Seriously, when a player has committed a no-no, the officials throw flags and blow whistles; fans cheer or boo; and after a brief huddle, the guy in the striped shirt turns on his microphone and announces to the crowd, and to you, exactly what the heck has just happened. He makes a little signal and tells you that number so-and-so, of the offense or defense, gets so many yards for whatever. For example, "Number 75, defense, fifteen yards for illegal use of the hands." He also does a funny little dance that symbolizes and kind of reenacts the infraction that was committed. The dance involves a lot of arm-waving and flapping. Each series of flaps means something, but we're not concerned because the ref also announces the penalty.

I think it would be cool to do just that to people on the street: "Hey, guy in the brown suit, ten yards for horking a loogie on Elm Street."

A penalty often results in loss of yards, which means that the team that committed the naughty act must move back a set number of yards. The team may lose five, ten, or fifteen yards. A penalty could also mean that the naughty team loses a down or that the good guys are awarded an automatic first down. Some penalties combine these punishments; it depends on the seriousness of the infraction. There are over a hundred penalties and rule violations. You don't need to know all of them because they are not only confusing but boring—with a giant, gold-plated "B." The most common penalties include the following:

Encroachment (Five Yards): Encroachment occurs when a player enters the neutral zone and makes contact with an opponent before the ball is snapped. Remember: no touchy-feely before the ball is snapped!

Offside (Five Yards): A player is offside when any part of his body is beyond his scrimmage or free kick line when the ball is snapped. I've called this penalty on more than a few dates.

Striking (Five Yards): Striking is the act of swinging, clubbing, or propelling the arm or forearm to whack an opponent. I've committed this penalty on more than a few dates.

Intentional Grounding (Ten Yards and Loss of Down): This refers to the ball, of course. It is illegal for the quarterback to save his own ass by simply throwing the ball away. If the passer is clearly going to get sacked for a loss and he decides to fling the ball down the field where none of his receivers has a realistic chance of catching it, the result is a ten-yard penalty and loss of a down. Intentional grounding will not be called when a passer, while out of the pocket and facing a loss of yardage, throws a pass that lands at or beyond the line of scrimmage, even if an offensive player does not have a realistic chance of catching the ball. This rule also applies when the ball lands out of bounds over the sideline or end line.

Clipping (Fifteen Yards): Clipping occurs when an offensive player blocks a defensive player from behind; jumping on, hitting, kicking, or generally mauling the defender from behind is a penalty. Sounds weasely enough to me. I'm amazed they even have to write rules for stuff like this. It's not even clipping. What the hell is clipping? I understand the league is also reviewing a new name for a penalty for running your cleats over your opponent's mother. They're considering calling it shredding, grating, or pureeing.

Unsportsmanlike Conduct (Fifteen Yards): Any act contrary to the generally understood principles of sportsmanship is considered unsportsmanlike. If you don't know the principles of sportsmanship, just remember that saying anything about anyone's mother is generally considered poor sportsmanship. Saying things like, "Nice tackle," to a guy who just tried to knock your spleen out your left nostril is good sportsmanship.

Roughing the Passer (Automatic First Down): Since quarterbacks can't run and hide, they need some protection. That's why it's illegal to nail the quarterback once he's released the ball. If an attacker hits the quarterback by accident (it's up to the ref to decide), then there is no penalty.

Pass Interference (Automatic First Down and Ball Placed at the Spot where the Foul Was Committed): This one is huge and can make the difference between a major, game-turning or even game-winning play, or a game-breaking, heart-wrenching turnaround. There are two types of interference: offensive and defensive.

Offensive pass interference occurs on a pass play when the receiver is afraid the ball is about to be intercepted by the defense. Consequently, the receiver boots the defender in the shnutz, or grabs him by the head or something.

Defensive interference is when a pass defender interferes with a receiver trying to catch the ball (as long as the defender could not have caught the ball himself). For example: a defender with his back to the ball sees that the receiver that he was covering is ready to catch the ball. If the defender pulls out a copy of *Playboy* and holds the centerfold up to the receiver's nose, therefore trying to distract him, this is interference.

If the contact between the offensive player and the defender was an accident or just a result of momentum, then interference is not called. Two guys colliding as they reach for the ball is incidental. A guy pulling a salmon from his pants and clubbing the receiver over the head with it is not incidental.

And you thought that there were no rules to football; that these guys could just run around and, at will, beat the living tar out of each other. Well, now you know the difference. You know what is allowed (you are allowed to pull someone down by the thighs and gnaw on their ankles) and what isn't allowed (driving your head through your opponent's intestines). It all seems rather civilized now, doesn't it? I bet all your apprehensions about the roughness of the game have just faded away like last week's bruises.

NFL Coaches: Drop and Give Me Fifty

The coach is in charge of the players; he is their off-field leader. A good coach is strong, and full of passion and wisdom. He must not only know everything about the game but also how to motivate his players. He is under enormous pressure; if his team doesn't put out, then he is put out—on the street. A coach works virtually year-round. He prepares practice schedules, game strategies, and play books—sometimes with more than 200 plays for the offense alone. He also makes free-agency decisions, scouts future draft picks, and monitors some training camps.

A coach is respected by his players but is often under fire from the owners and fans for his decisions. Coaching is a huge job, and the team's head coach works with a full coaching staff to get everything done. The full coaching staff includes the following: offensive coordinator, defensive coordinator, special team's coach, quarterback coach, offensive line coach, defensive line coach, linebacker coach, secondary coach, and the strength coach. A team may have even more coaches for specific positions, depending on how many coaches the team wants to pay for.

Hey, you can't talk about coaches without quoting the famous motivator Vince Lombardi. Hell, they named the Super Bowl trophy after the guy. Widely considered the best ever, Lombardi was a master of motivation and led the Green Bay Packers to five league titles, including the first two Super Bowls. But what better way to learn about Lombardi than to let you read his words yourself… Here are some snippets from the legend.

LOMBARDI'S CHICKEN SOUP FOR THE ASS-KICKIN' SOUL

"If you aren't fired with enthusiasm, you'll be fired with enthusiasm."

"You never win a game unless you beat the guy in front of you. The score on the board doesn't mean a thing. That's for the fans. You've got to win the war with the man in front of you. You've got to get your man."

"Confidence is contagious and so is lack of confidence, and a customer will recognize both."

"In great attempts, it is glorious even to fail."

"They may not love you at the time, but they will later."

"The harder you work, the harder it is to surrender."

"The difference between a successful person and others is not a lack of strength, not a lack of knowledge, but rather in a lack of will."

"It's not whether you get knocked down, it's whether you get up."

"Winning is not a sometime thing: it's an all the time thing. You don't win once in a while; you don't do the right thing once in a while; you do them right all the time. Winning is a habit. Unfortunately, so is losing."

"I firmly believe that any man's finest hour, the greatest fulfillment of all that he holds dear, is the moment when he has worked his heart out in a good cause and lies exhausted on the field of battle—victorious."

NFL Team Owners: "I Own Your Ass!"

The NFL may keep their eyes (and fingertips and purse strings) closely on the game of football, but it is the team owners who are putting the screws to the team itself. The owners are not only concerned with the proverbial bottom line, but they take care of the team itself. They hire and fire staff and players alike. The NFL may collectively own the game, but the individual owners own their team, its name, its history, and its future.

Who would own a football team? Generally, owners are people who want to be public figures, because they will certainly receive lots of attention, good and bad, for their decisions. They must also be sports fans, and they must love the game as much as they love trying to make money. Which leads us to the most important requirement to be an NFL owner—cash, tons and tons of cash. NFL franchises can cost in the hundreds of millions of dollars to buy; if that number makes you choke on your tongue, then maybe this is not the perfect gift for your guy next year.

The NFL is set up for the owners to make truckloads of cash, even if their team doesn't make it to the Super Bowl. The money end of the NFL is set up so that each team receives an equal share of the television revenue and splits the ticket sales 60:40. The idea is that even the suckiest team has a fair shake at making some cold cash. An individual team's revenues from local radio, luxury boxes, parking, concessions, and private seat sales are not shared with the other teams. The money made from NFL properties, the guys making the hats, T-shirts, and various other football junk that you hide deep in the closet, and the Super Bowl is shared. Being an owner sounds pretty sweet. I wonder if paying a player's salary means that he is at the owner's disposal at all times for all things? I bet I could find a few things for a couple of Greek-godlike studs to do around the house.

OWNER STORIES

Owning a team is not all power and glory; sometimes it takes a lot of creativity, courage, and big *cujones* to keep a team going. Here are a few of those stories.

Just Win… Please: Pittsburgh Steelers owner Art Rooney ran his team for thirty-nine years before they finally won him a division title.

Owner Puts the "Super"in Super Ball, Er, Bowl: For the first couple of years, the Super Bowl was far from super. The NFL champion Green Bay Packers made sure the upstart AFL champs never had a chance and laid the boots to them with authority. Super Bowl III was the turning point when Joe Namath and his underdog New York Jets—champs of the AFL—took on and beat the heavily favored, Johnny Unitas-led Baltimore Colts. That year marked the end of NFL domination and let fans know from then on it was anybody's game. It was also special because Kansas City Chiefs owner Lamar Hunt had an inspiration to change the name of the game from the "AFL-NFL World Championship" to the "Super Bowl." He got the idea while watching his daughter playing with an ultrabouncy "Superball."

"DO YOU LIKE YOUR JOB?" GENERAL MANAGERS

Owners can't always be around. So they hire general managers to run the show while they are off making money so they can afford a team of big oafs. GMs are often cold, calculating people because they have to make extremely difficult decisions for the owners. It is the general manager's job to decide who plays with the team, who's getting the boot, and how much the players will get paid. The GM also makes the final decisions in the draft, so he must work closely with the head coach to ensure that he is satisfying the team's needs. This guy keeps track of the front-office staff, too. After the owner, this guy's butt is the one to kiss.

The NFL: Big Brother is Watching

OMNIPOTENT

The NFL organization is mostly in charge. They own the game or at least are the dictators of the game. As with all dictators, the NFL is rakin' in the dough.

No pro sports league is more omnipotent or omnipresent than the NFL. They practically invented big business in professional sports. Think about it for a minute. Can you watch television for more than twenty seconds without seeing some kind of football imagery? Can you walk more than forty paces before seeing someone with NFL gear on either their head or their bosom? Nope. The NFL is everywhere and that is why they make so much moola. The organization doesn't make millions from its TV contracts—it makes billions. Sounds pretty sweet, but if you want to join the club, you'll be shelling out lots of dough. When the Jacksonville Jaguars joined the NFL in 1995, they paid a $200-million entry fee. The fee doubled by the time Cleveland joined in 1999. If you're looking for a piece of the pie, you'd better start saving your pennies.

The NFL is a powerful, almost mystical force. It's kind of like the Wizard of Oz, only instead of one guy behind a curtain, it is a whole bunch of people conspiring together to get a lot of money and, of course, to feed the passions of Americans who respect toughness, grit, courage, and hard-ass determination.

So, if you're a player in the NFL, this is how it works: the NFL owns the game of football in America, the owners own the team, the GM owns your job, the coach owns your life, and the officials own your ass if you break the rules that the NFL made up. The players may not own their game, their life, or their own asses, but they do own big, fat checks. Everyone is happy and everyone makes tons of money. Except for the officials, but no one likes them anyway.

Lions, tigers, and bears, oh my?

CONFERENCES, DIVISIONS, AND TEAMS OF THE NFL

With all the teams and all those silly names, the National Football League can be confusing. Let's get it straight right now. The NFL is divided into two conferences: the American Football Conference and the National Football Conference. Each conference is divided into three divisions: east, central, and west. Here is how it looks:

The American Football Conference (AFC)

East Division	Central Division	West Division
Buffalo Bills	Baltimore Ravens	Denver Broncos
Indianapolis Colts	Cincinnati Bengals	Kansas City Chiefs
Miami Dolphins	Cleveland Browns	Oakland Raiders
New England Patriots	Jacksonville Jaguars	San Diego Chargers
New York Jets	Pittsburgh Steelers	Seattle Seahawks
	Tennessee Titans	

The National Football Conference (NFC)

East Division	Central Division	West Division
Arizona Cardinals	Chicago Bears	Atlanta Falcons
Dallas Cowboys	Detroit Lions	Carolina Panthers
New York Giants	Green Bay Packers	New Orleans Saints
Philadelphia Eagles	Minnesota Vikings	St. Louis Rams
Washington Redskins	Tampa Bay Buccaneers	San Francisco 49ers

The best team from each conference meets for the Super Bowl. The actual playoff format is confusing and not very interesting. The important thing to remember is that each team only plays sixteen regular-season games plus a few preseason ones beginning in August, before the road to the Super Bowl begins. With so few games to base your team's performance on, each game is very important. The Super Bowl is held in January and is the biggest football event in the world.

How a Team is Created

I know how I would select a team: according to good looks, charm, hard bods, and stamina (of course). But building an NFL team is not quite as easy as this. Generally, a team must first make sure it has a solid quarterback, skilled running backs, and talented wide receivers. After this, player selections are based on each team's specific strategy. And where can you get such beautiful athletic specimens? Not at your corner grocery store (believe me, I've looked). Teams pick their players in the draft.

The NFL draft is an annual two-day event held in New York City in late April. It is televised on ESPN and is actually fun to watch. It is very exciting. Everyone is wheeling and dealing, dreams—and millions of dollars—are at stake, and the fans are there to add their two cents. It works like this: there are seven rounds and each team has one pick in each round; the team with the worst record from last year picks first, the team with the second-worst record picks second, and so on, leaving the Super Bowl winners to pick last. Each team is allowed fifteen minutes to make their selection in the first round and only five minutes in the following rounds.

The selections are made from the top college players in the country. About 2,500 players become eligible for the draft each year. Players courted by a team go through many physical and mental tests given by the coaches, scouts, and club officials. They are measured, weighed, put through skill-testing drills, given intelligence tests, and tested for illegal drug use. NFL security also does background checks on prospective selections and informs team officials of their findings. With so much at risk, teams are very careful with their draft selections.

stamina

Super Chuck Trivia Stud says: Want to stump your football guy? Ask him if a player can play in the NFL if he has not played at college first. The answer is yes. Joe Perry did. Joe never played beyond junior college before he joined the US Navy. While playing with the Navy team, he was discovered by the 49ers. When he left the Navy, lots of colleges made offers, but Joe went pro.

The Teams

There are a lot of teams in the NFL. Here are some quick summaries so you can recognize who you are watching. I won't give you any statistics on the teams because, well, they are boring. If you are interested in following a team as it progresses through the season, which is helpful in showing up your football guy, then pick up any football magazine. The writers love to include stats; I am more of a butt person myself.

THE AMERICAN FOOTBALL CONFERENCE

These are the teams that are in the AFC and their brief (sometimes really brief) histories.

BALTIMORE RAVENS

Team Colors: purple, black, and gold
Stadium: PSINet Stadium (grass)
Their Story: On February 9, 1996, football returned to Baltimore after an eleven-year absence. The team's name comes from a poem, entitled *The Raven*, by Baltimore's most famous resident, Edgar Allan Poe. The fans of the city chose the name through an elimination process that included focus groups and phone surveys. Two-thirds of the fans polled, that is, a whopping 33,288 people, picked "Ravens." Along with the new name came the new mascots: three mildly creepy ravens called Edgar, Allan, and Poe. The birds were born on August 24, 1998. A few weeks before their birth, three giant purple eggs were laid in a giant nest in the Ravens' stadium. There were 60,000 fans in the stadium one hot summer night when a loud rumble was heard. The rumbling got louder, and when fans rose from their seats to see what was happening, pieces

of eggshell began to fly through the air. When the egg shrapnel finally settled, three big birds dressed in Ravens uniforms popped out from the nest—lookin' mildly creepy.

BUFFALO BILLS

Team Colors: royal blue, scarlet, and white
Stadium: Ralph Wilson Stadium (artificial turf)
Their Story: Buffalo is famous for two things. First, it is the only team to play in (and lose) four straight Super Bowls. Second, it has incredible fan support. Since Buffalo was granted its franchise on October 28, 1959, Bills fans have shown overwhelming support—so overwhelming that their stadiums must constantly be expanded. Their first stadium was War Memorial Stadium. It was expanded from 26,000 to 45,748 seats within a few years. But that still wasn't enough room for all of Buffalo's crazy fans. In 1973, the team moved to Rich Stadium; then, in 1998, it moved to its present home, Ralph Wilson Stadium. The team also acquired a new mascot in 2000. His name is Billy and he is a big, blue, weird-looking buffalo. If you want to scare the crap out of kids at the next birthday party, you can hire Billy to entertain (call 716-648-1800 ext. 307).

CINCINNATI BENGALS

Team Colors: black, orange, and white
Stadium: Paul Brown Stadium (grass)
Their Story: In anticipation of their new NFL franchise, Cincinnati began constructing their team's stadium in 1966; it was scheduled to be completed in 1970. The franchise was granted to the city on May 24, 1967. The team played its first seasons in Nippert Stadium before moving into the brand-new one. The team name comes from a former football team that played in Cincinnati in the 1930s and 1940s. The Bengals' silly cheerleading squad is named the Ben-Gals (I guess it's better than the Ben-Gays).

CLEVELAND BROWNS

Team Colors: brown, orange, and white
Stadium: Cleveland Browns Stadium (grass)
Their Story: The Browns were born on June 4, 1944, when Cleveland businessman Arthur B. McBride was granted a franchise in the new All-American Football Conference. Their first season of play was in

1946. When the AAFC folded in 1949, the Browns joined the NFL. But that is not the most interesting part of their history. In 1961, Arthur B. Modell purchased the Browns for $4 million. Old Arty Boy then shocked everyone by announcing that he was moving the team to Baltimore in 1996. Browns fans and city officials freaked out. They began a campaign that was so loud that even the great NFL took notice. The NFL, in its infinite wisdom, provided the solution: they built Cleveland a new stadium and guaranteed that football would return to the city by 1999. Evil Arty then relinquished the "Browns" name, colors, and team history (thus becoming just plain old Arthur B. Modell again). In 1998, the new Cleveland franchise was granted to Al Lerner. The team began to play in 1999.

Weird Fact: Twenty former Browns coaches and players have become NFL head coaches.

DENVER BRONCOS

Team Colors: orange, navy blue, and white
Stadium: Mile High Stadium (grass)
Their Story: Like a few other NFL teams, the Denver Broncos are famous for their exceptional fan support. They have had record sellout crowds every year since 1970, with waiting lists every year. Denver was granted their franchise on August 14, 1959. The original owner was a bit strapped for cash after blowing all his money on the football franchise. To cut costs, he bought used uniforms for the team that included silly socks with vertical stripes. Two years later, when head coach Jack Faulkner took over, the socks were gathered and destroyed in a public burning ceremony. The amazing fan support began in 1965 when there were threats to sell the team. The team stayed in Denver, and fans showed their appreciation by buying 23,000 season tickets (under 8,000 were sold the year before).

Weird Fact: The coldest game in Denver history took place in December 1983. The temperature was 0° Fahrenheit with a windchill at –30° Fahrenheit. Brrrrrr.

INDIANAPOLIS COLTS

Team Colors: royal blue and white
Stadium: RCA Dome (artificial turf)
Their Story: The Colts have a dicey history. Follow me carefully. In 1947, a Baltimore Colts team was founded in the All-American Football

Conference. Three years later, when the dust settled between the AAFC and the NFL, the Colts became an NFL member. Unfortunately, the team failed, and the franchise went tits up after the 1950 season. Three seasons later, the city was whining for a team. The NFL commissioner set up a challenge: if the city could sell 15,000 season tickets in three weeks, then they could have the franchise back. The ticket sales actually took over four weeks, but the commissioner was a softy and the city got its franchise again. On January 23, 1953, Carroll Rosenbloom became the principal owner of the new Baltimore Colts. Then, in 1984, new owner Robert Irsay moved the team to Indianapolis, and the Indianapolis Colts were born.

JACKSONVILLE JAGUARS
Team Colors: teal, black, and gold
Stadium: ALLTEL Stadium (grass)
Their Story: Jacksonville really, really wanted football in their city. On August 17, 1989, Touchdown Jacksonville, a community group led by businessman Tom Petway, began stomping their feet for an NFL franchise. In September 1991, Jacksonville made its move. Loaded up with a $60-million commitment from the city to renovate their crappy Gator Bowl, they became one of eleven cities to apply for an expansion. Unfortunately, the NFL officials came to town to inspect the Gator Bowl. The NFL said that not only was the Gator Bowl a stupid name, but additional renovations were needed to meet NFL standards. Okay, maybe it was me who said that the Gator Bowl was stupid, but it is true that the NFL people were being sticklers for the standards. City council was unable to come up with a solution to their cash flow woes, and sadly Jacksonville had to withdraw from the expansion race. But dry your eyes, this story is not over. Due to the amazing community spirit in this fair city, a solution was found by city council—the money was now there to fix the "Stupid Name" Bowl. Jacksonville was back in the race, and they eventually received their franchise on November 30, 1993.

KANSAS CITY CHIEFS
Team Colors: red, gold, and white
Stadium: Arrowhead Stadium (grass)
Their Story: On August 14, 1959, a twenty-six-year-old Texan got pissed off. Lamar Hunt had politely asked the NFL for a franchise and was refused. Well, if the NFL wouldn't let him play in their league, then he

would start a league of his own. Lamar founded the American Football League (and made himself the president). In 1960, eight new teams began play in the new AFL. Hunt's new team was called the Dallas Texans. In 1963, the team was moved to Kansas and was renamed the Chiefs. They eventually joined the NFL in 1966 when the AFL merged with the NFL.

MIAMI DOLPHINS

Team Colors: aqua, coral, blue, and white
Stadium: Pro Player Stadium (grass)
Their Story: Miami was granted their franchise to the American Football League on August 16, 1965. In 1967, they became the ninth team to play in the AFL and joined the NFL in 1970. The Dolphins were the first team in football history to record a perfect season. In 1972, they won every game they played, including the Super Bowl.
Weird Fact: During their winning season of 1972, the Dolphins beat the New England Patriots in a game with a final score of 52–0.

NEW ENGLAND PATRIOTS

Team Colors: silver, red, white, and blue
Stadium: Foxboro Stadium (grass)
Their Story: An AFL franchise was awarded to Boston businessman Billy Sullivan Jr. on November 22, 1959. Billy named his new team the Patriots. In 1971, the team's name was changed to the New England Patriots, and they moved into their new stadium. After two name changes (I think these guys had some identity issues in 1971), the stadium was named the Foxboro Stadium.

NEW YORK JETS

Team Colors: green and white
Stadium: Giants Stadium (grass)
Their Story: Harry Wismer was granted his franchise in 1959. Harry named his team the Titans. Unfortunately, the franchise went bankrupt and was bought by a group headed by David "Sonny" Werblin in 1963. The group paid a million bucks for the penniless Titans and then changed their name to the New York Jets.
Weird Fact: Jets player Steve O'Neal punted the football ninety-eight yards in a game against the Denver Broncos on September 21, 1969, setting an NFL record that still stands today.

OAKLAND RAIDERS

Team Colors: silver and black
Stadium: Network Associates Coliseum (grass)
Their Story: Oakland was selected to receive an AFL franchise on January 20, 1960, to replace a Minneapolis team that had defected to the NFL. In 1982, they were moved from the Oakland Coliseum to the Los Angeles Coliseum in Southern California. After spending twelve seasons in L.A. (those poor buggers), the team was moved back to their original home.

PITTSBURGH STEELERS

Team Colors: black and gold
Stadium: Three Rivers Stadium (artificial turf)
Their Story: Until 1940, the Pittsburgh Steelers were the Pittsburgh Pirates. They were granted their franchise on July 8, 1933. Due to a shortage in manpower in 1943 created by the war, Pittsburgh combined its team with Philadelphia for the season. In 1944, they hooked up with the Cardinals to survive. In 1945, the team stood alone and became the team that we know today.

SAN DIEGO CHARGERS

Team Colors: navy blue, gold, and white
Stadium: Qualcomm Stadium (grass)
Their Story: On August 14, 1959, an AFL franchise was awarded to Los Angeles. Even though the Los Angeles Chargers played well in their first season, they did not have a lot of fan support. The team was moved to San Diego in 1961.

SEATTLE SEAHAWKS

Team Colors: blue, green, and silver
Stadium: Husky Stadium (artificial turf)
Their Story: On June 4, 1974, the Seattle Seahawks became the twenty-eighth member of the NFL. Since then, they have played a whole bunch of football games.
Weird Fact: Seattle coach Dennis Erickson once fined three of his players $1,000 for eating hot dogs during a preseason game.

TENNESSEE TITANS

Team Colors: navy, red, titan blue, and white
Stadium: Adelphia Coliseum (grass)
Their Story: The Houston Oilers became members of the AFL on August 14, 1959. Oilers owner and president K. S. "Bud" Adams Jr. was one of the founding fathers of the AFL. In 1968, the Oilers became the first team in football history to play in a domed stadium—the air-conditioned Astrodome. The Oilers had another first in 1997. That year the team was moved to Tennessee, becoming the first team to ever call that city home. The "Oilers" name was retired in 1999 and the team was renamed the Titans.

THE NATIONAL FOOTBALL CONFERENCE

Here are the teams that are in the NFC and a few words about them (mostly true).

ARIZONA CARDINALS

Team Colors: red, black, and white
Stadium: Sun Devil Stadium (grass)
Their Story: The Arizona Cardinals were born in 1994. Of course, that date does not mark the true beginning of the team. The first incarnation was in 1898, when a man named Chris O'Brien formed the Morgan Athletic Club in Chicago. The team then became the Racine Streets, and it was during this time that the owner bought some used uniforms from the University of Chicago. The old, faded clothes were described as "cardinal red." The team soon became known as the Racine Street Cardinals. It was 1920 when the American Professional Football Association, direct forerunners to today's NFL, came along and announced that there would be only one team in Chicago. At the time, the city also had a team called the Tigers. The two teams faced off to win the rights to the city, the fans, and the franchise. The Cardinals won, and the Tigers had their furry little butts kicked out of town. The Cardinals remained in Chicago until 1960, when they moved to St. Louis. In 1988, the team moved again—this time to Phoenix. Finally, in 1994, the team moved to Arizona and became the Arizona Cardinals.

ATLANTA FALCONS

Team Colors: black, red, silver, and white
Stadium: Georgia Dome (artificial turf)
Their Story: On June 30, 1965, Rankin Smith, a successful life insurance executive, shook $8.5 million out of his wallet and bought an NFL franchise. The Falcons became the first team in NFL history to have a year-round practice facility in 1978. The Georgia Dome became the Falcons' new home in 1991.
Weird Fact: On November 27, 1977, the Falcons were playing Tampa Bay. The Falcons only allowed Tampa Bay to gain seventy-eight yards total in that game.

CAROLINA PANTHERS

Team Colors: blue, black, and silver
Stadium: Ericsson Stadium (grass)
Their Story: A franchise was granted to the Panthers on October 26, 1993. The team's first season was in 1995, and they were very competitive. In fact, with a 7–9 season, the team set a record for most wins in the first year by an expansion team.

CHICAGO BEARS

Team Colors: navy blue, orange, and white
Stadium: Soldier Field (grass)
Their Story: Da Bears began their history in 1920 when the Stanley Starch Company of Decatur, Illinois, sponsored a football team. For a measly hundred bucks, the team joined the American Professional Football Association (which later became the NFL) on September 17, 1920. In 1921, the starch company gave permission for the team to be moved to Chicago, under the condition that the team keep the name "Stanleys" for one year. After that year was over, the team was renamed the Bears. The Bears were the first team to buy a player from another team when, in 1922, they paid $100 for Ed Healey from Rock Island. The Bears also played the first indoor game in football history in 1932. The team made Soldier Field their home in 1971.
Weird Fact: The team's most lopsided win happened during the NFL championship game in 1940, when they slaughtered the Washington Redskins in a 73–0 victory.
Lunkheaded Fact: Bears player Dick Plasman became the last player in the NFL to play without a helmet during the same 1940 game.

DALLAS COWBOYS

Team Colors: blue, metallic silver-blue, and white
Stadium: Texas Stadium (grass)
Their Story: A franchise was granted to Dallas on January 28, 1960. In 1966, they began their record-setting twenty consecutive winning seasons streak. This included eighteen years in the playoffs, thirteen divisional titles, and five trips to the Super Bowl. The Cowboys have won five Super Bowls, including Super Bowl VI, XII, XXVII, XXVIII, and XXX.

In 1967, the team announced that they would build their own stadium in Irving, Texas. On October 24, 1971, they moved into the 65,024-seat Texas Stadium.
Weird Fact: The famous Dallas Cowboys cheerleaders were originally called the Cow-Belles. I guess they scrapped the original original name, the Cow-Patties.

DETROIT LIONS

Team Colors: honolulu blue (this is the official listed color, I didn't make it up) and silver
Stadium: Pontiac Silverdome (artificial turf)
Their Story: After three unsuccessful attempts to establish football in Detroit in 1920, George A. Richards had a new idea. He would give up on getting a franchise for Detroit and instead try to get one for Ohio. He was awarded a franchise on July 12, 1930. Richards bought the Portsmouth, Ohio, Spartans and in 1934 moved their butts to Detroit. The Detroit Lions made their mark in football by scheduling a game on Thanksgiving Day. This tradition has been maintained, except for a five-year break from 1939 to 1944. So, if you want to blame anyone for the fact that your guy becomes a belligerent, beer-bloated buffoon every Thanksgiving Day, you can lay the blame on the Detroit Lions organization.

GREEN BAY PACKERS

Team Colors: dark green, gold, and white
Stadium: Lambeau Field (grass)
Their Story: Green Bay is the third-oldest team in the NFL. It began its history in 1919, when the Indian Packing Company sponsored a football team. Now we know that the team was named after its original backers. The team was granted a franchise in the new NFL on August 27, 1921. One of the really interesting things about this team is that they are in a city of less than 100,000 people and are the only community-

owned, nonprofit organization in the NFL. They are also well-known for their famous coach, Vince Lombardi.

MINNESOTA VIKINGS

Team Colors: purple, gold, and white
Stadium: Metrodome (artificial turf)
Their Story: Only the Dallas Cowboys have made more playoff appearances than the Vikings. Their franchise was first awarded to them by the AFL in August 1959. In January 1960, the five Minnesota businessmen that owned the team bailed on their AFL membership to attain an NFL franchise. In 1982, the team moved from the 40,800-seat Metropolitan Stadium to the Hubert H. Metrodome (63,000 seats).

NEW ORLEANS SAINTS

Team Colors: old gold (once again, I didn't decide the gold was old), black, and white
Stadium: Louisiana Superdome (artificial turf)
Their Story: On All Saints' Day (November 1) in 1966, the NFL announced that New Orleans had been awarded a franchise. So when it was declared that the new team was called the Saints on January 9 of the following year, no one was surprised. The Saints first played in the Tulane Stadium and in 1975 moved to the Superdome.
Weird Fact: In 1985, New Orleans Saints coach Bum Phillips was replaced by his son, Wade. Bum was so hated by Saints fans that Wade thought he needed some help to take the heat off. He jokingly started a rumor that he was adopted.

NEW YORK GIANTS

Team Colors: blue, white, and red
Stadium: Giants Stadium (grass)
Their Story: Tim Mara went to New York to visit a fight manager to buy an interest in Gene Tunney's contract. Instead, he came home with an NFL franchise that he bought for $500 in 1925. By the end of his Giants' first season, he had invested $25,000 into the team. That was a lot of clams in those days. Tim kept the team in the family. His sons, Jack and Wellington, succeeded him. Tim Mara II served for many years as the team's vice president. Preston Robert Tisch bought 50 percent of the club in 1991; he now serves along with Wellington Mara as the team's co-chief and as an executive officer.

PHILADELPHIA EAGLES

Team Colors: midnight green (what the hell is that?), silver, and white
Stadium: Veterans Stadium (artificial turf)
Their Story: A franchise was granted to Bert Bell and Lud Wray on July 8, 1933, in Pittsburgh. The team wasn't the Eagles then, of course; they were the Frankford Yellow Jackets and they cost $2,500. In 1941, one of the biggest game of "tradesies" took place. Philadelphia's and Pittsburgh's owners traded clubs, and Alexis Thompson became the new owner of the Eagles. In 1943, when the war drained the ranks of the football league, Philadelphia and Pittsburgh combined teams for one season. The team was known as both the Phil-Pitts and the Steagles. The strange team had two co-coaches for the season: Greasy Neale (Eagles) and Walt Keislung (Steelers). The team returned to normal the following season as the Philadelphia Eagles.

ST. LOUIS RAMS

Team Colors: Rams navy blue and Rams gold
Stadium: Trans World Dome (artificial turf)
Their Story: St. Louis is one of the NFL's older franchises, beginning their life in Cleveland in 1937. The team played for six seasons before they had to disband for one year due to the war. Dan Reeves bought the team in 1941 and moved them to Los Angeles for the 1946 season. In 1972, the Baltimore Colts' owner, Carroll Rosenbloom, traded franchises with the Rams owner, Bob Irsay. Carroll Rosenbloom was now the new owner of the Rams. In 1979, Rosenbloom died, and the team's new owner/president was the widow Rosenbloom, Georgia. In 1995, the Rams moved from their home in Los Angeles to St. Louis and began play in the Trans World Dome.

SAN FRANCISCO 49ERS

Team Colors: 49ers gold (yup, their very own shade) and cardinal
Stadium: 3Com Park at Candlestick Point (grass)
Their Story: On June 4, 1944, a franchise was granted to San Francisco by the All-American Football Conference, and their first season was in 1946. The team joined the NFL in 1950 after the AAFC went kaplooee. The famous and remarkable Joe Montana played for them during the 1980s. The 49ers join Dallas in winning five Super Bowls: XVI, XIX, XXIII, XXIV, and XXIX.

TAMPA BAY BUCCANEERS

Team Colors: Buccaneer red (again with their own shade), pewter, black, and orange
Stadium: Raymond James Stadium (grass)
Their Story: On April 24, 1974, Tampa became the NFL's twenty-seventh franchise. Tampa holds the NFL record for most consecutive losses: twenty-six games before the losing streak was broken on December 11, 1977. They won some games, too.

WASHINGTON REDSKINS

Team Colors: burgundy and gold
Stadium: FedEx Field (grass)
Their Story: George Preston began the Redskins' history in 1932 when he bought an inactive Boston franchise. The team was originally named the "Braves" because they played in Braves Field (home of the Major League Baseball team). In 1933, the team was moved to Fenway Park and was renamed the Redskins. Four years later, the team moved to Washington, D.C., and played in Griffith Stadium. It was in this year, 1937, that the Redskins acquired a marching band and a fight song; these were both firsts for the NFL. In 1944, the Redskins had another first when they formed their own radio network to broadcast their games. The Washington Redskins hold the NFL record for most consecutive sellout seasons. The streak began in 1966 and is still alive today.

There, now you know who's who, where they are, and what they've been up to. It's kind of like your high school reunion—only none of these guys got fat.

What is so super about it?

LEGENDS AND LORE OF FOOTBALL'S HOLY GRAIL

On one Sunday every January, year after year, the world shuts down. Millions of chickens lose their wings, nachos are drowned by the bagful in gobs of cheesy goo, and beer is poured down the throats of most of the nation's adult (sort of) males. The big whoop-de-do festival of booze, gas, deep-fried pork products, and other assorted salty snacks is driven by thirty-four years of momentum. It's Super Bowl Sunday, and it's every guy's perfect excuse for a party.

If you're going to become a football fan, Super Bowl Sunday is the best place to start. It's the one game of the year that everyone is watching—whether they're a football fan or not. And with such a huge crowd, you won't be alone in your lack of football savvy. In fact, if you've been reading this book so far, you probably know more than the average beer guzzler kicking back in his La-Z-Boy and using his belly as a snack tray.

Super Sunday: Pregame Hype

If you watch football for the first time on Super Bowl Sunday (also known as just "Super Sunday"), you're in for a treat. For starters, the game doesn't start until early evening, but the pregame show kicks off at about noon. All day and into the evening you can watch and listen to ex-players, ex-coaches, and fat guys who just like to be near ex-jocks yack about football. They'll talk a little about the upcoming game, telling you who will win and why. They'll talk about every Super Bowl that's ever been played, who won, and why. They'll talk about all the teams that aren't in the Super Bowl and why. And, if you listen really closely, near the end of the pregame show they'll even talk a little about how to get rid of watermarks on the coffee table and some surefire techniques for getting rid of bikini-line bumps—just to see if the nation is paying attention.

Just being in the same room with those commentators trying to fill six hours of airtime is going to fill your head with some football smarts. Even if you're reading a book or getting the snacks ready, you're bound to absorb some new football knowledge by osmosis. Here's a hint, though: don't use words like "osmosis" at your party. Stick to one-syllable words on Super Sunday. Pass, beer, ref, and jerk immediately come to mind.

Beyond the Game: Other Entertainment

After wasting, er, spending, an entire day listening to ex-football players talk about the upcoming game, you're in for another treat. If you aren't quite sure about the technicalities of the game but just want to be there for the party, there's still plenty to keep you entertained, starting with the national anthem.

THE STAR-SPANGLED BANNER

With the world watching, the singing of *The Star-Spangled Banner* at the Super Bowl has become an event in itself. The list of past singers is a musical who's who, and the anthem offers you a taste of the excitement and fanfare of the big day. The list of patriotic past performers includes Marvin Gaye, Charlie Pride, Cheryl Ladd, Diana Ross, Barry Manilow, Neil Diamond, Billy Joel, Whitney Houston, Harry Connick Jr., Garth Brooks, Natalie Cole, Kathie Lee Gifford, Vanessa Williams, Luthor Vandross, Jewel, and Faith Hill. Even more astonishing is the list of megastars who were turned down as anthem singers. William Shatner (thank God), Conrad Bain, Bernie Koppel, and Howard Cosell have all been given the brush-off by the person in charge of anthem singer selection and jock-strap laundering.

THE HALFTIME SHOW

After a little bit of football, it will be time for the halftime show—always a huge extravaganza of singing, dancing, and fireworks. Sometimes, as you watch the halftime show, you might think, "What is this crap?" In Super Bowl XXXIV, when these big stick-figure puppet creatures were walking around, I thought, "What the hell?" Then one of my beer-soaked fellow fans pointed out that it was a dramatization of how the world would be a better place if the various nations and cultures would celebrate their differences and join together in the spirit of harmony and love. Then he stuck a pretzel stick in each nostril and pretended he was a warthog—for the next ninety minutes.

DON'T TOUCH THAT DIAL

Even if you've never watched a Super Bowl game before, you may have tuned in for the commercials. Each year commercial airtime gets more and more expensive, and advertisers look for maximum bang for their buck by producing commercials that will be the talk of the watercooler on Monday morning. So central are Super Bowl ads to television history that The Museum of Radio and Television even showcased them in a screening called "The Super Bowl: Super Showcase for Commercials." Some of the most memorable Super Bowl ads include:

1984: The first and the best mega-ad. This commercial launched the Macintosh computer with a creative, dramatic ad based on the George Orwell novel about Big Brother and the Thought Police. It remains the most acclaimed television ad of all time.

Showdown: In this ad, basketball legends Michael Jordan and Larry Bird bet a Big Mac on who could come up with the most fantastic hoop.

The Bud Bowl: This commercial for Bud versus Bud Lite featured little beer bottles sporting football helmets and competing annually for the Bud Bowl title. Maybe it's funny when viewed through beer goggles.

The Bud Frogs: Bud and the Super Bowl go hand-in-hand, and this ad, featuring the three frogs croaking, "Bud, Weis, Er," was one of America's favorites. Later, it featured lizards, jealous of the frogs' celebrity. This was a hit as well.

"Stinkers"

The game itself... well... it usually sucks. Oh, there have been some good ones, including the 2000 Super Bowl when Tennessee came within a yard of tying St. Louis on the last breathtaking play of the game. But, too often, the Super Bowl is a Super Blowout and the winner lays on a pounding so convincing the game is over after the first half. But, still, millions watch. The Super Bowl is America's unofficial national holiday, and despite the potential testosterone overdose, it's a great occasion to get together with some friends, have a few cocktails, and watch a whole lot of men in tights.

Super Bowl Super Facts

Here are a few Super Bowl facts that you should know, just in case your guy wakes from his drunken stupor and starts asking questions.

FIRST BROADCAST

When the Super Bowl was first televised in 1967, it was actually shown by two networks—NBC and CBS. It was the first and only time in history that rival U.S. networks broadcast the same game. This was permitted only because the first meeting between the NFL and AFL champions was considered historic.

A TRADITION IS BORN

The Super Bowl hasn't always been so super. In fact, it hasn't always been known as the Super Bowl. Up until Super Bowl III, in 1969, the Super Bowl was simply called the AFL-NFL World Championship Game—not exactly a ratings grabber. Kansas City Chiefs owner Lamar Hunt coined the name Super Bowl after he watched his daughter playing with a Superball. Inspiration struck and Hunt jumped on it. An institution was born.

KNOW YOUR ROMAN

Of course, it would be too simple to call the Super Bowl the 2000 Super Bowl or even Super Bowl 34. Inspired, I guess, by Sylvester Stallone's Rocky series, the Super Bowl uses Roman numerals. This system wasn't so bad to start with, but now that we're in the thirties, it's getting a tad cumbersome. But then I guess the Roman feel gives the game more of a gladiator kind of appeal. It's a little corny, but, hey, when I turn XXXVI-II, I might start using Roman numerals, too, just to confuse people.

THE FIRST REAL SUPER BOWL

With a new name promising an extraordinary game, the NFL needed some excitement for its first so-called Super Bowl. Super Bowl III was held in Miami in 1969. Despite the fact that the two previous championships had been called the AFL-NFL World Championship Game, they were back-dated as Super Bowls. So, when the championship was renamed and the first official Super Bowl was held, it was actually called Super Bowl III. In the previous two championships, the Green Bay Packers had knocked the snot out of the American Football League's best—first the Kansas City Chiefs, then the Oakland Raiders—35–10 and 33–14 respectively. For two straight years, 1967 and 1968, the big game was a big joke, and the AFL champs weren't holding up against the more established NFL teams. In the first-ever Super Bowl in 1969, it looked like another AFL team was being led to the slaughter, as the New York Jets were matched against the mighty Baltimore Colts. The Colts were favored by seventeen points.

The Jets' playboy quarterback, Broadway Joe Namath, didn't believe the hype. He didn't think his team was outmatched at all. In an interview leading up to the first Super Bowl game, Namath uttered the words that would either make him the championship's greatest hero or biggest goat. "We're going to win Sunday," he said. "I guarantee you." Not the kind of quote players are supposed to toss out to inspire the opposition.

Namath's guarantee is a textbook example of what you'll never hear an athlete say today. These days they stick to the boring, "We'll give 110 percent and leave everything out on the field and, God willing, the best team will come out on top. And no one will get hurt except maybe the mascot and we don't much care for him anyway."

More astounding than Namath's guaranteed victory was that he actually came through on it. The underdog Jets won 16–7, and Namath secured his place as one of the legends of the game.

Chuck Chinwaggin':
Namath wasn't the only one to make boastful promises. Isaac Bruce, wide receiver for the Rams, shot off his mouth in August 1999, before the Rams even played a game and when they were a 200-1 long shot to win the Super Bowl. He said, "When I'm well, I'm hell. And I'm well." The Rams won, and the boastful poet Bruce caught the winning touchdown.

Broken Leg? Tape Two Aspirin to It

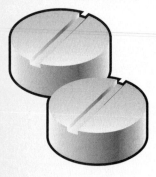

It takes more than a little boo-boo or a broken nail to keep a real football player out of the big game, and there's no better example of football fortitude than Jack Youngblood. The defensive end for the Rams broke his left leg in the last half of a 1979 playoff game against the Cowboys. He was taken to the locker room, X-rayed, and diagnosed with a broken fibula. Tape it up, he told the doctors. They tried to explain that a broken leg can't be taped. Youngblood wasn't buying. "Tape two aspirin to it," he told them. The doctors taped him up and he finished the game. Then he went out the next week and played in the NFC championship game. Two weeks later, Youngblood played in the Super Bowl against the Pittsburgh Steelers. The Rams lost, but not for lack of effort. Youngblood described the pain as "like having a knife stuck in the side of your leg constantly." Like, uh, how would he know that? But the pain was worth it, he said. "You cannot miss an opportunity to play in the Super Bowl."

Another poster boy for workers' compensation is Ronnie Lott. In the final game of the 1985 season, Lott smashed his pinky between his own helmet and Dallas running back Tim Newsome's chest. He, too, was told by doctors he couldn't play, and he, too, sought a second opinion—his own: "Fix it up so I can play," he said. He played and Lott's 49ers lost 17–3. A month later, his finger hadn't healed and he was given a choice: either amputate the tip of his pinky or do a bone graft. He chose the chopping block and the pinky was still a little sensitive. "But so what," he said.

History of the Super Bowl

To know the Super Bowl of today, you need to know your big-game history. So here are the winners, losers, and MVPs, as well as the locations and the attendance of each Super Bowl up to the year 2000. I have translated the Roman numerals into arabic numerals, just in case your football guy wants to read this section. I know that we girls are sufficiently advanced in our cerebral evolution, but our dear guys... let's just leave it at that.

YEAR	WHICH ONE	WHO'S PLAYING	MVP	ATTENDANCE
2001	XXXV (35) in Tampa	Baltimore 34, N.Y. Giants 7	Ray Lewis	71,921
2000	XXXIV (34) in Atlanta	St. Louis 23, Tennessee 16	Kurt Warner	71,253
1999	XXXIII (33) in Miami	Denver 34, Atlanta 19	John Elway	74,803
1998	XXXII (32) in San Diego	Denver 31, Green Bay 24	Terrell Davis	68,912
1997	XXXI (31) in New Orleans	Green Bay 35, New England 21	Desmond Howard	72,301
1996	XXX (30) in Tempe, Arizona	Dallas 27, Pittsburgh 17	Larry Brown	76,347
1995	XXIX (29) in Miami	San Francisco 49, San Diego 26	Steve Young	74,107
1994	XXVIII (28) in Atlanta	Dallas 30, Buffalo 13	Emmitt Smith	72,817
1993	XXVII (27) in Pasadena	Dallas 52, Buffalo 17	Troy Aikman	102,000
1992	XXVI (26) in Minneapolis	Washington 37, Buffalo 24	Mark Rypien	63,130
1991	XXV (25) in Tampa	N.Y. Giants 20, Buffalo 19	Ottis Anderson	73,813
1990	XXIV (24) in New Orleans	San Francisco 55, Denver 10	Joe Montana	72,919
1989	XXIII (23) in Miami	San Francisco 20, Cincinnati 16	Jerry Rice	75,179
1988	XXII (22) in San Diego	Washington 42, Denver 10	Doug Williams	73,302
1987	XXI (21) in Pasadena	N.Y. Giants 39, Denver 20	Phil Simms	101,063
1986	XX (20) in New Orleans	Chicago 46, New England 10	Richard Dent	73,818
1985	XIX (19) in Stanford	San Francisco 38, Miami 16	Joe Montana	84,059
1984	XVIII (18) in Tampa	L.A. Raiders 38, Washington 9	Marcus Allen	72,920
1983	XVII (17) in Pasadena	Washington 27, Miami 17	John Riggins	103,667

YEAR	WHICH ONE	WHO'S PLAYING	MVP	ATTENDANCE
1982	XVI (16) in Pontiac, MI	San Francisco 26, Cincinnati 21	Joe Montana	81,270
1981	XV (15) in New Orleans	Oakland 27, Philadelphia 10	Jim Plunkett	76,135
1980	XIV (14) in Pasadena	Pittsburgh 31, L.A. Rams 19	Terry Bradshaw	103,985
1979	XIII (13) in Miami	Pittsburgh 35, Dallas 31	Terry Bradshaw	79,484
1978	XII (12) in New Orleans	Dallas 27, Denver 10	Harvey Martin and Randy White	75,583
1977	XI (11) in Pasadena	Oakland 32, Minnesota 14	Fred Biletnikoff	103,424
1976	X (10) in Miami	Pittsburgh 21, Dallas 17	Lynn Swann	80,187
1975	IX (9) in New Orleans	Pittsburgh 16, Minnesota 6	Franco Harris	80,997
1974	VIII (8) in Houston	Miami 24, Minnesota 7	Larry Csonka	71,882
1973	VII (7) in Los Angeles	Miami 14, Washington 7	Jake Scott	90,182
1972	VI (6) in New Orleans	Dallas 24, Miami 3	Roger Staubach	80,591
1971	V (5) in Miami	Baltimore 16, Dallas 13	Chuck Howley	79,204
1970	IV (4) in New Orleans	Kansas 23, Minnesota 7	Len Dawson	80,562
1969	III (3) in Miami	N.Y. Jets 16, Baltimore 7	Joe Namath	75,389
1968	II (2) in Miami	Green Bay 33, Oakland 14	Bart Starr	75,546
1967	I (1) in Los Angeles	Green Bay 35, Kansas City 10	Bart Starr	61,946

How to Get to the Super Bowl

The road to the Super Bowl is a tough one, with many barriers to cross and many challenges to overcome. First, you have to find tickets, and the $350-plus to pay for them. Then, you have to buy a plane ticket, find a hotel room in the host city, and make it alive to the game after a full week of Super Bowl partying. Oh, and there are a few challenges for the players, too.

FIRST MAKE THE PLAYOFFS

The journey to the Super Bowl starts with baby steps. Before a team can dream of clutching Vince Lombardi's ball (that's the Super Bowl trophy, sicko), they must first make the playoffs. The most surefire way to secure a place in the postseason is for a team to win its division after the sixteen-game regular season. But first, here's a breakdown of how the playoffs work. The NFL is divided into two conferences, the American Football Conference and the National Football Conference. The Super Bowl features the AFC champ against the NFC champ. To get to the playoffs, a team can either win the AFC or NFC East, Central, or West division, or it can sneak in as a "wild card" team. The wild card teams are the three nondivision-winning teams from each conference with the best win/loss records for the season. If a team doesn't win their division title or a wild card spot, they had better start calling the scalpers 'cause it's the only way they're getting to the big game.

Wild Card Weekend: The first weekend of the playoffs is known as "wild card weekend" and features two games in each conference. One game pits two wild card teams against one another, and the second game features the third wild card team and the division winner with the worst record of the three division winners. The winners of these games survive for the next playoff round.

Conference Semis: The next round is the conference semifinals. With two wild card weekend survivors and two division champs left in each conference, these teams play off, and the two winners move on to the AFC and NFC conference championships.

Conference Finals: Some real football fans believe the two conference final games are even better than the Super Bowl because they feature teams from the same conference battling for their playoff lives. The same-conference thing adds fuel to the fire because conference rivals play each other more often than the Super Bowl opponents. In other words, the two teams that meet in the Super Bowl know very little of one another, but the teams in the conference final games go way back. And they hate each other's guts. Makes for some good football.

The Big Game: After surviving the conference finals, the winners are rewarded with a trip to a sunny city (or at least a city with a domed stadium), accommodations in a nice hotel, media attention, public adoration, and a shot at football's coveted prize—the 6.7-pound, 20.75-inch-tall silver football on a pyramid stand, known as the Vince Lombardi Trophy after the legendary Green Bay Packers coach who guided his team to victory in the first two Super Bowls. Where the big game is held is decided by the NFL. Since hosting a Super Bowl means a huge infusion of cold cash to the host cities, many cities salivate at the mere mention of Super Bowl Sunday. To decide who gets the game, each city sends in a bid to the NFL tooting their own horns and offering to cover many of the league's expenses (like accommodations, travel, and in-room-full-contact-jello-massages).

Super Bowl Losers and Winners

The Super Bowl is a proving ground for those who aspire to have their names etched in football history. Super Bowl winners will always have a special place in NFL lore, while losers will either be forgotten or known as the guys who couldn't win when it counted. Maybe it's not fair, but it sure cranks up the intensity level on the field.

Most of the attention leading into the big game is on the quarterbacks. They're the team leaders, and usually they're the guys who can win or lose a game themselves. Quarterbacks have to see the whole field, and decide in seconds whether to run or pass and who to pass to. If they don't decide, they get driven into the ground by one or more 300-plus-pound men named Bubba. If they do get the pass off, quite often they are still driven into the ground, just because they didn't get the pass off quite fast enough.

Winning quarterbacks are heroes, losers are goats. That's just the way it is. Take John Elway, now retired from the Denver Broncos. He's now known as John Elway, one of the greatest, perhaps *the* greatest, quarterback ever. He definitely gets the award for best teeth for a quarterback. He can be considered the greatest because he put together a brilliant career capped by two Super Bowl titles in 1998 and 1999.

But before those wins, Elway was known as three-time Super Bowl loser John Elway. His Broncos were beaten by the New York Giants in Super Bowl XXI and then by Washington the next year. A few years later, Elway and his Broncs returned to the big show but lost to San Francisco. He still had a great career and made it to the big game three times, but ultimately he was considered a loser. No matter what else he did in his career, he couldn't win the one game that counted most.

Fortunately, Elway polished up his good name with those two wins to go with his three losses. Buffalo Bills quarterback Jim Kelly was not so fortunate. He, too, put together a great career, but his name will forever come attached with the title "Super Bowl Loser." You've gotta feel sorry for the guy, really. Four times he made it to the big one, and four times he had to deal with defeat. Minnesota and Denver have all lost four Super Bowls, but only Kelly can claim to have QB'd four losing teams.

Dan Marino is another great loser. This guy could really make a pass and is considered one of the best ball chuckers in the history of the world. But he retired without ever winning a Super Bowl. He only ever played in one—in 1985, when the Dolphins lost to the San Francisco 49ers.

RISING TO THE OCCASION: SUPER BOWL HEROES

Some players just seem to have a knack for bringing their big games to the big games. There are many more heroes than are listed here, but this list is a good place to start. Here are some of the Super Bowl's more legendary performers.

JOE MONTANA, SAN FRANCISCO 49ERS, QUARTERBACK

Four wins, three MVP awards, and the ultimate quarterback name. There couldn't be a better pickup line than, "Hi, I'm Joe Montana."

One of his most shining of many shining moments came in Super Bowl XXIII. With 3:10 left to play, Montana's Niners were down 16–13 and had the ball ninety-two yards from the end zone on their own eight-yard line. Completing eight of nine passes in an eleven-play drive, Montana led his team to within scoring distance. With a ten-yard pass to John Taylor, Montana pulled off one of the greatest comebacks in football and provided a thrilling end to a mostly boring, touchdown-free game.

TERRY BRADSHAW, PITTSBURGH STEELERS, QUARTERBACK

Two straight wins (Super Bowls XIII and XIV), two straight MVP awards. After watching the bald loudmouth on FOX football broadcasts, I can't believe it either. But, hey, I always give credit where it's due.

EMMITT SMITH, DALLAS COWBOYS, RUNNING BACK

MVP of Super Bowl XXVIII, with 132 yards rushing, twenty-six yards in pass receptions, two touchdowns, and a ton of blocks—all with a painful separated shoulder that needed surgery to be put back together. Who'd have thought a guy named "Emmitt" could be so tough.

KURT WARNER, ST. LOUIS RAMS, QUARTERBACK

His MVP award in Super Bowl XXXIV and record 419 yards passing in the game capped the most improbable season in NFL history. Warner was supposed to be the St. Louis Rams' backup QB until a preseason injury to high-priced starter Trent Green thrust Warner into the spotlight. Before becoming a big-game, big-league hero, Warner was an undrafted, unwanted ballplayer who couldn't even make it in the Arena Football League. Warner went from stocking shelves in a grocery store (when no football team wanted him after college) to being named the best player in the biggest game in the world.

"THE HOGS," WASHINGTON REDSKINS

Redskins Hall of Fame coach Joe Gibbs has won three Super Bowls with three different quarterbacks (Joe Theismann, Doug Williams, and Mark Rypien). It's an amazing feat, and at least some of the credit should go to the big guys who protected those passers—"The Hogs." Joe Jacoby, Russ Grimm, and Jeff Bostic kept defenses at bay in all those games and were unsung heroes. Today, their posters hang at all-you-can-eat buffets nationwide under the caption "Banned!"

BART STARR, GREEN BAY PACKERS, QUARTERBACK

The MVP of the first two Super Bowls was considered a machine or a "push-button" quarterback because of his efficiency and accuracy.

BILL WALSH, SAN FRANCISCO 49ERS, COACH

A master of offensive football, Coach Walsh led the Niners to three Super Bowl championships in three appearances before stepping down following his team's victory over the Cincinnati Bengals in Super Bowl XXIII. Having a guy like Joe Montana in the lineup made life easier for Walsh. In fact, a waffle iron could have likely led Montana, Jerry Rice, and the rest of the San Fran greats to victory.

THE GREATEST TEAMS

Want to start a good argument at a Super Bowl party? Just bring up the subject of the greatest team ever. In baseball, it's hard to argue against the Yankees and all their championships. Same goes for hockey's undisputed all-time champs, the Montreal Canadiens. But football is a little different. For one thing, the Super Bowl only goes back thirty-five years, while pro football NFL-style has been around for eighty. A few teams have emerged as Super Bowl dominators, while other franchises have shown flashes of brilliance but no stamina. Here's a rundown of some of the best teams. Use this to pick your favorite or to throw a little gas on the fire you started by bringing up this topic in the first place.

SAN FRANCISCO 49ERS

Who can argue? Five appearances in the Super Bowl, five titles. They've done it with two different quarterbacks and two different coaches. They're a lousy team right now, but Niners fans have much to be proud of and a lot of bragging rights. A high point has to be the back-to-back wins in Super Bowls XXIII and XXIV.
Names of Note: Joe Montana, Jerry Rice, Ronnie Lott, and Steve Young.

GREEN BAY PACKERS

Lombardi's boys won the first two Super Bowls and captured their place in football history. Fans with long-term memory loss were treated to title number three when Brett Favre (Far-ver-ah) led the Pack to a win in Super Bowl XXXI over the New England Patriots. This time, though, there was no repeat.

Names of Note: Vince Lombardi, Bart Starr, Paul Hornung, and Brett Favre.

PITTSBURGH STEELERS

These guys were as big a part of the 1970s as John Travolta and Fonzie. With back-to-back Super Bowl wins in 1975 and 1976, then again in 1979 and 1980, the Steelers may have been the greatest in a decade of great teams.

Names of Note: Terry Bradshaw, Lynn Swann, Mean Joe Greene, and Franco Harris

DALLAS COWBOYS

Okay, move over Steelers. "America's team" won a pair of Super Bowls in the 1970s, too. Unfortunately, they also lost a pair, both to Pittsburgh. Advantage Steelers. But the Cowboys enjoyed a renaissance in the 1990s with three titles in four years, tying the Niners with five Lombardi trophies. And one of those victories was over the Steelers. Advantage Cowboys. Hmm... this does get interesting.

Names of Note: Roger Staubach, Harvey Martin, Randy White, Emmitt Smith, Troy Aikman, and Michael Irvin.

MIAMI DOLPHINS

By virtue of their perfect season in 1972, capped by a Super Bowl win over Washington, "The Fish" make the cut. They are also repeat champs with a win over Minnesota the following year. The Dolphins also have three Super Bowl losses.

Names of Note: Don Shula, Larry Csonka, "The No-Name Defense," and Dan Marino (perhaps the best quarterback never to win a Super Bowl).

Gambling on a Winner: You Can Bet on it

As I have mentioned, Chuck and I would never condone or participate ourselves in any kind of gambling because we understand (thanks to a helpful lecture... um... I mean discussion with Chuck's wife) that gambling is not only silly and wasteful but perhaps displays questionable moral judgment. That aside, I will pass on to you what some football fans, excluding Chuck and me, do for added excitement during the Super Bowl.

Any good Super Bowl party will include a Las Vegas element with some friendly wagers. You can bet on almost anything with the Super Bowl, starting with who will win the coin toss to who will catch the first pass, score the first touchdown/field goal, make the first interception, or recover the first fumble. You can bet that certain receivers will catch over or under a certain number of passes, or you can bet on how many yards the quarterbacks will throw the ball. Creative gamblers can even throw in outside elements to spice up the game. In past Super Bowls, you could wager whether the winning Super Bowl team would score as many points as Michael Jordan would score in that day's basketball game. Or you could bet which would be greater: the number of points scored by the winners or the number of beers consumed by your buddy Larry. When you place a few small-time bets with friends, the game will be more exciting, and your wager will keep you glued to the set even if one team surges to a lopsided win.

> The Omniscient Chuck: Don't bother consulting the stars, the tea leaves, or tarot cards. In 1979, twelve "gifted" psychics predicted the outcome of the Super Bowl between the Dallas Cowboys and Pittsburgh Steelers. Nine of them insisted Dallas would win easily. Pittsburgh won 35-31.

Legends, Lore, and Myth

As one of America's biggest celebrations, the Super Bowl has also generated its share of urban legends, folklore, and myths. The following are some of the stories that have circulated about the Super Bowl. They all have one thing in common—there is no truth or fact to them whatsoever.

- Water systems in major cities are brought to the brink of collapse each year due to the mass flushing at Super Bowl halftime.
- Disneyland becomes a ghost town on Super Sunday and

lines for rides (if there are any) move briskly. Same goes for golf courses where tee-time reservations are normally needed—you can just walk on.

- Two-thirds of the world's avocados are sold around the Super Bowl for use in guacamole dip.
- One-half of all heart attacks are recorded on Super Bowl Sunday.

Super Bowl Party Essentials

If you have already witnessed an official Super Football Guys Super Bowl party, you are already aware of the disgusting cheese-dripping, fat-soaked, originally-lived-in-a-can type of hors d'oeuvres served at such a gathering. Personally, I'd rather pack a secret picnic in my pocket for these events, but since we are attempting to become true football fans and are immersing ourselves in its culture, we must experience an official Super Bowl party to its full extent. This will involve preparing for your friends, and even perhaps digesting, food that comes from a recipe beginning "Shake can well before opening." To plan an authentic Super Bowl party, I have called upon our resident football guy extraordinaire. Take it away, Chucky Cheese.

Chucky Cheese: "You can't have a good Super Bowl party without the right food. Absolutely no petit fours, no quiche, and vegetables are only tolerated if deep fried in batter or accompanied by a fatty dip. Baseball may call for hot dogs and cracker jacks, but that's kid stuff compared to a Super Bowl feast. For any Super Bowl party there are a few staples: beer, pizza, beer, nachos, beer, chili, and beer.

CHUCKY'S CROWD PLEASIN' RECIPES

Here are a few recipes for some easy, crowd-pleasing Super Bowl snacks. Pass these on to your guy and tell him to get cookin'.

RANDY HOGGE'S GARLIC WIENIES

Want to be a thoughtful, food-bearing party guest but don't really want to spend any cash? For a cost-efficient dish, cook up a batch of garlic wienies. They are so simple to prepare, you don't even need a recipe. Just cut up a package of wienies and place them in a slow cooker along with a jar of your favorite garlic sparerib sauce. Cook them for a few hours, or even all day, and make sure you mention to everyone how long it took to cook them. That way, they'll be fooled into thinking this is a real snack and not just a bunch of old hot dogs.

CHUCKY'S ULTIMATE CHICKEN WINGS

These wings aren't just spicy, they're tasty, too.

Chucky's Ultimate Chicken Wings

a bunch of wings	1 tsp. (or more) of butter
1/4 cup of Frank's Red Hot Sauce (or more if you like 'em real hot and spicy)	1 tsp. of cider vinegar
	ketchup (to taste)
1 tbsp. of oil	

Step one is to cut up your wings. This is the least fun part of the operation. Separate the upper and lower wings, and remove the tips. Also, I like to cut away that little webby-thing of fat that joins the two sections. Once you finish hacking and whacking, fry those babies. I use a deep fryer because it's safer than a pot of oil, but I suppose you could use a deep frying pan. You could also bake the wings (at 350°F for about twenty minutes), but baking is for wussies. Once fried, mix your saucy ingredients in a big pan. Toss the cooked wings in, mix them around, and let them warm and absorb that sauce. Serve with carrots, celery, and blue cheese dressing.

CHUCKY'S QUICK AND EASY NACHOS

There's no better, easier snack than nachos with cheese. I find microwaving is actually better than the oven when making nachos. All you need to do is layer a plate full of nachos with grated cheddar or fancy-pants Mexican-flavored nacho cheese. Make sure you cover all the chips or you'll have fights on your hands. Nuke 'em until the fromage melts, and serve with salsa and sour cream. For more elaborate nachos, you can also add some cooked hamburger, tomatoes, green peppers, onions, or jalapeno. But remember, too much fussing will take up more of your valuable couch-riding time.

DON'T FORGET WET-NAPS

CHUCKY CHILI

Chili is a sacred food for football fans, and most people have their own special, top-secret chili recipe. It's one of those foods that can be personalized and that cooks take great pride in preparing, serving, and bragging about. Everyone likes their own chili the best, and no matter what recipe you create, or how long you spend in the kitchen, they'll always say, "It's good. Not as good as mine, but good." That's why I do things the easy way. My chili recipe starts with some ground beef and a little envelope of premade chili spices. Throw in some water, tomato sauce, corn, or any other veggies you like, and you've got a utilitarian chili that tastes good normally and great when guests are tipsy and starving.

MOOSE DROPPINGS (MEATBALLS IN BEER SAUCE)

When beef and beer join forces in one dish, it's kind of like when Batman and Superman team up in a comic. Here's what you need:

Moose Droppings
2 lbs of ground beef, moose, elk, buffalo, venison, or any other roadkill that you have hanging around the grill of your car
2 eggs
1 cup of bread crumbs
2 tbsp. of onion flakes
salt and pepper
1 dozen beer (you only need one for the recipe, but it is always good to have backups just in case)
3 cups of ketchup
2 tsp. of onion salt
2 tsp. of Worcestershire sauce
In a large bowl, mix your meat with the eggs, bread crumbs, onion flakes, and salt and pepper. Roll your balls and broil them (turning them once) until they're a light brown. In a slow cooker, heat up the beer, ketchup, onion salt, and Worcestershire sauce. Add the meatballs to this mixture and let them cook for a few hours.

Chuck Tackles the Fat

If you're on a health kick—or have survived a six pack of heart attacks—you can still pretend to be clogging your arteries with fatty goodness while actually eating and drinking to your good health. Here's how to tackle the fat.

Eat a healthy pregame meal. Don't spend the first half of the game stuffing yourself with empty calories. Go ahead and eat that pizza, chili, or whatever else you were saving for halftime. You'll fill up and eat less through the day.

Drop the booze. While such a move may not wash with traditionalists, it will save you hundreds of calories. If you want to fit in with the beer-slugging boys, don't bother bringing a juice bar to the party. But if you want to eat healthy and watch the Super Bowl (a revolutionary concept), drink juices instead of soft drinks or beer.

Snack light. If you must shovel food into your face all day, shovel salsa and veggies instead of chips and dip, nachos and cheese, chicken wings, deep-fried cheese… ugghhhh… good luck.

If you haven't had a heart attack from just reading Chuck's recipes, you now know what to expect when you get invited to a Super Bowl party. If you can stomach this garbage, then you are a much heartier gal than me. If you are like me, then I suggest you bring that pocket picnic and just nibble on the party snacks when your host is looking. If you are the hostess, you can use some of the recipes from Chucky "King of Cheese," but just hide some veggies under the chili bowl. Even with the increased chance of heart attack or stroke, I do suggest attending Super Bowl parties. Super Bowl Sunday is the highlight of the season. It's a daylong event full of festivities. And if all else fails and the game sucks, at least you have tons of beer around, so booze it up, sister.

Why tempt fate?

I don't even like to think of all the lucky underwear, T-shirts, ties, caps, and other various stinking junk out there that is hauled out each year in the name of team spirit. Players, coaches, and fans do some very weird things to show their support for a team. Here are a few rituals that you already know, some that you don't know, and some that you'll wish you could forget.

Player Pranks

You think your football guy is weird? Take a look at some of the strange pranks that players do in the name of tradition and good luck.

A COLD SHOWER

It is a universal football image: the dumping of buckets of water on players or coaches after the big game. It is always a good prank, but in 1955, the coach of the Baltimore Colts, Weeb Ewbank, had enough of his sopping-wet players. Coach Ewbank announced that the next player to dump cold water on another player would be fined $1,000. You would think that losing a grand would be enough to stop players from playing this silly game, but no. Veteran players Gino Marchetti and Carl Taseff couldn't resist. The plan was to douse rookie Alan Ameche when he entered the locker room. The two cohorts had worked out a plan. Marchetti was to signal Taseff when the rookie was about to enter, and Taseff was to dump the bucket when Ameche opened the locker-room door. What Taseff didn't know was that Marchetti had turned on him and changed the plan. Marchetti signaled, the door opened, Taseff dumped the water, but it was not the rookie who entered. It was the coach, Weeb Ewbank, who received the cold shower. Luckily, the coach had a sense of humor and not only accepted the players' apologies, he also waived the fine.

HEAD CREAM

Fred Smerlas used to enjoy playing a common football prank over and over again. He often filled the helmets of his Buffalo Bills teammates with shaving cream. Smerlas thought this was hilarious. I think he had too much time on his hands.

HOT PANTS

Another common locker-room prank is the old atomic-balm-in-the-jockstrap trick. Usually, players are wise to this one and check their jock before they put it on. But, every once in a while, a player will forget or be in a hurry and get a bad case of "crotch on fire."

Lyle Blackwell, who once played for Miami, pulled this one off successfully on teammate Robert Sowell. Poor Robert was late for a team meeting one day and came rushing into the locker room and hastily pulled on his gear. The moment the jock hit his body, he knew what had happened. So did everyone else. An agonizing scream echoed through the room, and probably through the streets of Miami. Robert's first instinct was to try and wipe the ointment off, which only rubbed it in deeper. Then he ran for a cold shower, which only made the burning sensation hotter. When the meeting was over (and the screaming had subsided), the team found Robert Sowell on the trainer's table with two ice bags on molten... um... molten manhood. Needless to say, Robert missed practice that day. When he later joined his team, he was embarrassed to show them the trainer's chosen method of treatment. Nonetheless, he pulled down his underpants and out popped a hand. It waved at his teammates like it hadn't seen them in years. The trainer had filled a surgical glove with cooling lotion and taped it to Robert's... um... ruby-red jewels. I bet when Robert was getting late that day, he didn't expect to spend the whole practice with someone else's hand down his pants.

A Shoe Thing

We are not the only ones with a little shoe problem, girls. Football players seem to be quite superstitious about theirs. Defensive lineman Bubba Smith had a strange shoe ritual he performed before each game. Smith would put on and lace up his left shoe before putting on his pants. This meant that he had to struggle to pull on those oh-so-tight pants (need any help, darlin'?) over a size fourteen shoe.

Bubba wasn't alone when it came to a shoe fetish. A star player in the 1930s, Johnny "Blood" McNally, would lace up his shoes skipping every other hole for luck.

Bug's Bad Day

The story of the Houston Oilers of the late 1980s is a long series of practical jokes, but we will start somewhere in the middle with their kicker, Greg Montgomery.

To pay Greg back for an earlier stunt, his teammates wrapped him in tape and made a lovely "football mummy." But, of course, Greg had to pay them back for his payback. So, after the team abandoned the pile of tape formerly known as Greg Montgomery to go to practice, Greg took his revenge. He freed himself from the tape confines and proceeded to cut every chin strap and shoelace he could get his hands on. When the team returned and had to spend time replacing straps and laces, they had plenty of time to plan another counterattack.

They decided to hit Greg where it hurt—in his good-luck charm. The punter's charm was a ratty old stuffed Bugs Bunny that he kept in his locker, and every week he pinned on an obscene note insulting the Oilers' upcoming opponent. The next day, Greg opened his locker to find his dear Bugs Bunny cut open with the telltale scissors sticking out of the stuffed animal's back. Greg was mortified, but he lovingly taped Bugs back together and replaced the message with one aimed at his teammates. Two days later, another hit was put out on Bugs. This time, Greg found him hanging from the kicking net, where a shotgun had blown the bunny's head off. Ouch! This time, Greg was upset. He left Bugs there, and planned to wear a black armband and play taps at the next game. But, later, when the Oilers lost an important game against the Cleveland Browns, Greg removed Bugs Bunny from the post and repaired him, hoping to restore the magical charm. He didn't care if Bugs was full of buckshot, he needed his bunny; the team needed his bunny.

WIFE'S OFFENSIVE LINE

It is not just the actions of football players that cause strange payback behavior, sometimes a player's wife can yack too much. It all started rather innocently when a few of the players' wives got together for a baby shower. As usual, when you get a group of us gals together in a room, the conversation inevitably turns to the guys and their numerous shortcomings.

It was Minnesota Vikings kicker Rich Karlis's wife, Dena, who complained too loudly. Dena said that she didn't like the offensive line, the offensive line was a bad influence on her innocent hubby, and they were a bunch of slobs. In fact, she said that, since he started hanging out with those gorillas, Rich had let his personal grooming slide and was not dressing as fashionably as before. Were there repercussions to her allegations? Hell, yes.

At the next practice, the linesmen were waiting. Rich was later discovered (with his hands taped to his feet), blindfolded, gagged, and strung up upside down from the crossbar. A note announcing his offense was pinned, right side up, to his jersey. It read, "Wife talked about offensive line." Good thing she didn't finish her complaints that the offensive line also smelled and ate like pigs. She may never have found her hubby!

Coach Weirdos

Players are not the only ones to play practical jokes or display odd behavior in the name of good luck. Coaches have been known to act rather strangely, too.

HAT TRICK

Longtime, great coach of the Green Bay Packers, Curly Lambeau had a strong superstition. Curly believed it was bad luck for anyone on his team, including himself, to wear the same hat more than once. This wasn't a problem for Curly because he had a tendency to get very excited during a game and tear his hats to shreds.

DEAD TICKETS

As coach of the Atlanta Falcons in the early 1990s, Jerry Glanville had some very strange traditions. For example, Jerry liked to leave free tickets to the game at the gate. Sounds very thoughtful, but no one ever claimed the tickets. Why? Because the tickets were left for Elvis Presley, James Dean, and Buddy Holly. Once, in New York, Jerry left a special pass for the Phantom of the Opera.

Fandom: Large Groups of Weirdos

Fans will go to extreme lengths to support or protest their team. Face-painting and screaming like a maniac are both child's play compared to some stuff serious (or should I say, seriously mad) fans do.

BAD HEAD DAY

The late 1970s were not a good time for the New Orleans Saints. By 1980, they were really sucking; they lost their first twelve games of the season. Finally, their fans lost hope and showed their team shame in a poignant manner. For the home games, the fans sat in the stands with brown paper bags on their heads. Apparently, they were too embarrassed to be recognized as Saints fans, but they still had to show their support.

GIRL POWER

The power of football not only rules the lives of male fans. In 1980, football was a priority for women, too. The League of Women Voters rescheduled a presidential debate because it conflicted with *Monday Night Football*. The future of your country versus a game of football, and football wins? I don't know, girls.

SAVE THE BUNNIES

Politics is not the only thing that has been put aside for the sake of football. Sometimes, it is the lives of innocent little bunnies. No, I'm not referring to dear old Bugs.

In 1982, the farmers of Boise, Idaho, were plagued by thousands of crop-chewin' bunnies. The farmers had finally had enough and planned a massive bloody massacre to eliminate the bunnies once and for all. Luckily, the farmers accidentally planned the rampage for the same Sunday in January as the Super Bowl. Of course, the Super Bowl is more important than the crops, and the bunnies were spared. So, for the winter of 1983, thousands of fat Peter Cottontails hopped contently over the fields of Idaho. The country lived without potatoes, but the farmers didn't miss the big game.

FANS PROTEST

Sometimes the fans' devotion can be tested. Sometimes fans will meet the test and endure a team's bad year. But what happens if the fans' devotion has to endure fifteen bad years? Well, fans get pissed off. In December 1978, New York Giants fans had had enough. It had been fifteen years since the Giants had won a championship, and they were tired of cheering for the losing team. In protest, the fans hung owner Wellington Mara in effigy during a game. When that wasn't enough, they lit a bonfire with their season tickets. They tried suing the management for nonsupport and tried renaming the team the New York Gnomes. The fans even hired a plane to fly above the stadium pulling a giant banner that said, "15 yrs. Of Lousy Football. We've had enough." When they caught sight of this banner, 52,000 fans rose to their feet and, in unison, chanted that they'd had enough.

Unfortunately, none of these shenanigans worked. The New York Giants finished the season with a 6–10 record (that's six wins, ten losses, just in case your football guy asks).

"I'M NOT COMING IN UNTIL... "

Giants fans are not the only fans to protest a losing streak. In 1994, two Denver Broncos fans decided to take it upon themselves to inspire their team to help end a four-game losing streak. The two fans, Daren Trapp and Walt Dalton, announced that they would sit on the roof of their local bar in Colorado until the Broncos won a game. The two brave (stupid) fans endured icy rain and winds for five days until the Broncos finally beat the Seattle Seahawks on October 9, 1994.

WHOOF WHOOF

In 1984, Cleveland Browns cornerback Hanford Dixon named his defensive unit the "Dawg Defense." He began barking outlandishly at his opponents and encouraged the fans near the end zone to do the

same. We all know that fans don't need much encouragement to act like rabid fools. Soon the seats near the end zone became known as the "Dawg Pound," and fans showed up dressed in dog costumes. But, eventually, even this behavior was not weird enough—so fans began throwing dog biscuits and fake doggie doo on the field.

In October 1989, the barrage of barking and biscuits flying from the stands finally became too much for referee Tom Dooley. The Browns were playing against Denver, and the referee lost his patience with the "Dawg Pound." To avoid the cantankerous canines, he moved the game to the other end of the field. This change got Denver away from the barrage, but it also put the wind at the Browns' back for most of the second half and gave them an unfair advantage. With a wind-assisted field goal, the Browns won the game 16–13.

Chuck's Chatter: This was not the only time that unruly Browns fans forced a game to be moved to the other end of the field. In 1978, in a game against the Houston Oilers, Browns fans threw snowballs, cans, and bottles from the stands. Officials moved the play, and again the game was decided by a field goal. This time, the fans did not help the Browns—the Oilers made the field goal and beat the Browns.

DON'T MAKE ME USE THIS

Pittsburgh Steelers fans have a terrifying good-luck charm they use to show support for their team. This charm has been a staple in all games and has helped the Steelers to win Super Bowls IX, X, XIII, and XIV. What is this powerful object that inspires fear in all other teams? A towel. The "Terrible Towel" is black and gold, and waving it drives the fans wild.

FOOTBALL STRIPPER

December 12, 1954, was to be the legendary Crazy Legs Hirsch's last game. After the game, Hirsch was swarmed by 500 crazed fans looking for a souvenir. The fans ran at him, pulled at his jersey, and tried to tear it from his body. Afraid of being torn to shreds, he told the fans that he would remove it himself. He took off the jersey and threw it to the crowd. But still the rabid fans were not satisfied. So he removed the laces from his shoulder pads and tossed them. Still the fans wanted more. By the time Hirsch had finished, he was practically naked and wore only his padded shorts.

Ironically, Hirsch changed his mind about retiring and played three more years. When he finally decided to retire, he made certain to announce the news after the season was over.

WINNING LOSER

Fans are usually viewed as a bit crazy, but sometimes they can be sweet (or at least have a sense of humor about the whole thing). In 1975, the Balboa Boat Club of Newport Beach, California, started a strange tradition. Each year they gave the Lowsman Trophy to the college player who was picked last in the NFL draft. The winner of the trophy was given a banquet, a regatta in his honor, and other prizes. I'm not too sure this is a real honor, though. The trophy itself depicts a football player reaching down to pick up the ball that he's dropped. Not exactly a vote of confidence!

Big, Fuzzy Mascots

For the most part, mascots are cute and loveable. Sometimes they are mildly creepy, but the team and its fans seem to love them nonetheless. Mascots seem to be as well loved by the fans as the players, but not quite as loved as the cheerleaders. Here are a few stories of some of the NFL's mascots—from the cute to the creepy and back to the downright silly.

WHO-DEY

Who-Dey is a big, orange, smiling tiger and the mascot for the Cincinnati Bengals. He is my favorite mascot, and I think that he is the cutest thing in the NFL. Who-Dey has been with the Bengals for six seasons, and his favorite book is *Where the Wild Things Are*. His favorite song is "Welcome to the Jungle." Who-Dey better watch out because he is sooooo cute that I want to squeeze him to death!

T.D.

T.D. is the Miami Dolphin's mascot and he is a big, football-helmet-wearing dolphin. I think this guy is pretty cute, too. Take a look at his bio:

Pro: Entertains fans at all Dolphins home games… enjoys performing in front of large crowds and is great with kids…. One of the best prospects ever signed by the Dolphins, looks forward to a long and prosperous career with Miami.

College: Was an all-Atlantic Coast Conference pick at Atlantis University…. Majored in Marine Biology…. Mascot for both the football and the water polo teams.

Personal: Single…. Lists *Moby Dick* as his favorite book, *Jaws* as his favorite movie, and *Flipper* as his favorite show… enjoys sea diving, surfing, and playing pool.

Too cute.

T-Rac

You can't talk about mascot cuties without mentioning the Titans' T-Rac. He is a big, fuzzy raccoon, and he is adorable. Here are some of his hobbies: drag racing in his chariot, hiking, fishing, watching cartoons, space travel, and getting Titan-size hugs. Sweet!

Kinda Creepy: Freddy Falcon

Most of the mascots are big, fuzzy cuties, but sometimes teams do produce some creepy-looking things. They seem to be especially talented at creating creepy bird mascots. Maybe the teams should give up trying to make bird mascots; I don't think that they translate well. The Atlanta Falcons have a strange bird called Freddy Falcon. Freddy looks like he is always scowling, and when he does the "Dirty Bird" dance after a touchdown, I feel icky. But Freddy is a Gerber baby compared to Arizona's Big Red, the cardinal. I've had nightmares about that guy.

Big Red, the Cardinal

The Arizona organization tried to fool us by listing Red's favorite foods as birdseed and gummie worms. They also think that he will sound cute if they tell us that his favorite song is "The Bird Is the Word." But the word on this bird is "scary." I think he eats small children for lunch!

BILLY THE BUFFALO

Birds are not the only strange beasts on the field. Billy the Buffalo of the Bills makes my heart race. He's blue! A blue buffalo? He looks like he's choking to death. Someone call an ambulance! If you are interested in the story of how the Bills got him, check out their team site. It is a sad saga of a shunned blue buffalo and a kind stranger. It still doesn't make me like him.

SOUR DOUGH SAM

Sour Dough Sam (the mascot for the San Francisco 49ers) is my pick for the silliest mascot in the NFL for two reasons: (1) Sam is a goofy, brown-bearded hillbilly in a big hat and shoes, and (2) he's named after a type of bread (unique in football and perhaps in all sports). Sam's hobbies are listed as fans and cheerleaders (I'd like to know what a seven-foot mascot with a nose the size of my head plans to do with a cheerleader). Sam has been featured on *Football on FOX*, *Monday Night Football*, *SportsCenter*, *Extra*, *Evening Magazine*, MTV, and Nickleodeon.

Girls, now you understand that your football guy is not alone in his strange habits (except for that feather, waffle iron, and whipping cream trick; that's just plain sick). Players, coaches, and even us fans do some strange stuff in the name of team spirit. Even the team mascot can be a little wacky—and now you know which ones you should cuddle and which ones you should not make eye contact with.

Who's attached to those tight pants?

THE PLAYERS THAT YOU'VE JUST GOTTA KNOW

Okay, girls, you've heard their names as much as I have. There are some players from the past who you just can't ignore. There are also some players from the present who you just can't keep your eyes off.

Together, Chuck and I tried to come up with one list of players that all fans should know. We both based our choices on those qualities in a player that we feel are most important. However, I quickly noticed that Chuck had made some bad choices; he missed out on some of the best butts in the NFL today. When I informed him of his mistake, he did not take the criticism well. After hours of debate (which his wife eventually broke up with the garden hose), we came to a solution: we would make two favorite players lists. You will find our lists later in this chapter, but, first, my sisters, there are a few notable names from the past that you really must know. You will recognize their names from your football guy's constant yacking, and soon you will understand why they are famous.

Ten Blasts from the Past that You've Just Gotta Know

There are a few more that your guy probably babbles about, but these are probably the most famous.

JOHNNY UNITAS
1956–72: Baltimore Colts
1973: San Diego Chargers
Quarterback

The Pittsburgh Steelers picked up Johnny in the ninth round of the 1955 draft. Then, the Pittsburgh Dummies cut him. Johnny played semipro ball for a year before he was signed by the Baltimore Colts. It has been said that before Johnny, the Colts were nothing. He proved to be a perfect passer, and Pittsburgh had to kick themselves in the butt. Johnny became most famous for throwing touchdown passes in forty-seven straight games, and Pittsburgh kicked themselves forty-seven times. His signature trademarks were his high-top black shoes and his crew cut.

You may recognize him from such films as *Any Given Sunday* or the 1976 movie *Gus*.

JOE NAMATH
1965–76: New York Jets
1977: Los Angeles Rams
Quarterback

Joe is famous for two things besides just being one of the best quarterbacks in football's history. First, Joe not only made the American Football League respectable, he made it a serious threat to the NFL. In 1965, he was drafted by both the NFL and the AFL. Joe decided to go with the AFL's team, the New York Jets. The Jets offered him $450,000, which was then a record salary for a quarterback. The second thing that Joe is famous for is his public guarantee that his team, which was the underdog, would beat the heavily favored Baltimore Colts in Super Bowl III. The Jets did win, and Joe went down in history as a cocky son of a bitch.

Joe was as much a player off the field with the ladies as he was on the football field. He was a stud who loved the New York nightlife, which earned him his nickname, "Broadway Joe."

You may recognize him from such films as *Going Under*, *NFL Monday Night Football*, or *Chattanooga Choo Choo*. He has also appeared on the following television shows: *The Simpsons*, *Married with Children*, *The A-Team*, and *Sonny and Cher*. Namath also did several commercials, including ones for Ovaltine, Noxema, popcorn machines, and panty hose.

TERRY BRADSHAW
1970–83: Pittsburgh Steelers
Quarterback

The Pittsburgh Steelers weren't doing so well when they picked Bradshaw as the number-one draft pick in 1970. Luckily, Terry was very good, and took the team to four Super Bowls in the 1970s, winning them all. Terry was twice voted MVP and always rocked in the big games. Of course, Terry wasn't very popular with the opposition and was often bad-mouthed. Thomas "Hollywood" Henderson of the Dallas Cowboys said before the Super Bowl game against Pittsburgh that Terry Bradshaw "couldn't spell 'cat' if you spotted him the 'c' and the 'a.'" Terry didn't help his cause when he was quoted as saying, "I'm not afraid to let people know that I'm kind of an idiot."

You may recognize Terry from such films as *Cannonball Run* or *Smokey and the Bandit II*. He has also appeared on the following television shows: *Larry Sanders Show*, *Married with Children*, and *Everybody Loves Raymond*.

JOE MONTANA
1979–92: San Francisco 49ers
1993–94: Kansas City Chiefs
Quarterback

He may not have been the biggest guy or have had the most impressive arm, but Joe Montana got the job done. He led the 49ers to four Super Bowl wins and was named MVP three times. When Joe returned to football to spend his final two years with the Chiefs, he continued to be an amazingly accurate passer and showed no signs of slowing down.

JOHN ELWAY
1983–98: Denver Broncos
Quarterback

He was bigger, stronger, and faster than any of the quarterbacks before him. Elway proved that size does matter, because he could outrun and outreach everyone. He took the Denver team to the Super Bowl three times but couldn't win any of them alone. When the Broncos added the great running back Terrell Davis to the team, Elway ended his career with consecutive Super Bowl wins.

Elway was bitten by the acting bug and played himself in the movie *The Extreme Adventures of Super Dave* in 2000. He is currently the Broncos' director of pro scouting.

JIM BROWN
1957–65: Cleveland Browns
Running Back

Jim was voted rookie of the year in 1957 and MVP in 1958 and 1965. He never missed a game in his nine seasons. Using his star power, Jim worked to rehabilitate young gang members in Los Angeles.

He also used his star power to retire at the age of thirty so that he could pursue an acting career. You may recognize him from such films as *Rio Conchos, The Dirty Dozen, Dark of the Sun, The Split, Ice Station Zebra, El Condor, The Grasshopper, Slaughter, Black Gunn, I Escaped from Devil's Island, The Slams, Three the Hard Way, Take a Hard Ride, Fingers,* and *The Running Man.*

GALE SAYERS
1965–71: Chicago Bears
Running Back

Gale Sayers only played sixty-eight professional football games in his life, but in that short time he became a legend. Sayers was an elusive runner with amazing balance. His career was shortened by knee surgery in 1968; after the surgery, he wasn't able to perform to his former standards. Gale Sayers is also famous for the 1971 television movie *Brian's Song,* written about his friendship with teammate Brian Piccolo.

WALTER PAYTON
1975–87: Chicago Bears
Running Back

Payton could carry a ball and run like the wind. He missed only thirteen games in his career, and only because his coach forced him to take time off to let an ankle injury heal. You may have recognized Payton when he made a guest appearance on the television show *Coach* in 1995. In an unfortunate turn of events, Walter "Sweetness" Payton died of a rare liver disease in 1999 at the age of forty-five.

JOE GREEN
1969–81: Pittsburgh Steelers
Defensive Lineman

"Mean Joe" was Pittsburgh's number-one draft choice in 1969. Joe was a physically dominating player who was the heart and soul of his team. He was part of the famous "Steel Curtain" defense in Pittsburgh. Joe played in four Super Bowls and was defensive player of the year in 1972 and again in 1974. You probably would remember him from that famous Coke commercial in 1980 where a really cute little boy gives Green his bottle of Coke, and Green gives the boy his game jersey.

DICK BUTKUS
1965–73: Chicago Bears
Linebacker

"If you want to know the truth, I never liked any of the NFL players I butted helmets with. Not even when the game ended," said Dick Butkus in the introduction to *75 Seasons: The Complete Story of the NFL.*

Dick isn't a really nice guy, but he was one hell of a linebacker. He was big for his time and knew how to use his size to his advantage. He was the master of his domain in the middle field and demolished anyone who got near him. He averaged 12.6 tackles per game; in contrast, today's players would be very happy with ten tackles per game. Dick played only six healthy years for the Bears before he screwed up his knee and spent the next three years limping with the team. He was said to be the ultimate collision player.

Dick Butkus has done a lot of acting. He has been in many movies, including *Any Given Sunday, Necessary Roughness, The Last Boy Scout,* and *Gremlins 2: The New Batch.* He has had a regular role in the television series *Hang Time, My Two Dads,* and *Star Games.* He's made numerous guest appearances on other shows, including my favorite, *Wonder Woman.*

TEENA'S TOP TEN NFL STUDS

Girls, this is the list to really know. I have spent hours ogling, drooling, and fantasizing to bring you this list. When I began my research, I quickly noticed what would prove to be a problem. The NFL is chockfull of hotties, so I had to come up with a very selective process to make this list. I discovered what I call the "NFL Stud Selection Theory." The formula is as follows:

$$ToB + \$\$ + T \times OS = NFL \text{ Hottie}$$

That is, tightness of butt (ToB) plus the player's yearly earnings ($$) plus player talent (T) times the overall studliness factor (OS) equals an NFL Hottie.

Applying this revolutionary theory, I have come up with the following list.

DALE CARTER

Sign: Sagittarius
Born: November 28, 1969
Hometown: Covington, Georgia
College: Tennessee
Team: Denver Broncos
Position: Cornerback
Number: 40
Draft Date: 1992
Draft Team: Kansas City Chiefs

The first time I saw this guy, an irrepressible "Aaawwwww" escaped from my lips. Dale is adorable. He doesn't just look sweet but actually is sweet. When asked in an interview who the most impressive person he ever met was, Dale answered, his mother. Awwwww! In the same interview, he said that if he had to lose all his possessions except one, he would want to keep his little poodle. Awwww!

Dale is one of the top cornerbacks in pro ball today. He is also one of only two players playing today to have scored a touchdown on a punt return. He still lives in his hometown of Covington, Georgia, and is single. Dale Carter is so sweet I could eat him with a spoon.

BRETT FAVRE

Sign: Libra
Born: October 10, 1969
Hometown: Gulfport, Mississippi
College: Southern Mississippi
Team: Green Bay Packers
Position: Quarterback

Number: 4
Draft Date: 1991
Draft Team: Atlanta Falcons

Brett Favre personifies the great American quarterback. Aside from his obvious talent, he is good looking, smart, and charitable. Plus, get this, he even married his college sweetheart. Brett is used to being a star; he had his high school and his college jerseys retired. He started the Brett Favre Fourward Foundation, with three youth-oriented charities in Green Bay and Mississippi as the foundation's benefactors—Special Olympics, Cystic Fibrosis, and the Boys and Girls Club. This guy even spent Thanksgiving with the Salvation Army in Green Bay and Gulfport, Mississippi, donating food baskets to needy families. Brett Favre is good, very good. His hobbies include basketball, golf, and fishing. He also does a little acting; you may have caught him in *There's Something About Mary*.

STEVE MCNAIR

Sign: Aquarius
Born: February 14, 1973
Hometown: Mount Olive, Mississippi
College: Alcorn State
Team: Tennessee Titans
Position: Quarterback
Number: 9
Draft Date: 1995
Draft Team: Houston Oilers

With those piercing brown eyes, Steve McNair is an NFL stud. He is so good-looking that I cringe every time I see the defense going after him. Athletic talent runs in his family. Steve's brother is a quarterback for the Arena Football League Florida Bobcats. Steve is still close to his mom, Lucille. He splits his time between Nashville and his hometown. His mom nicknamed him "Monk" for his agile, monkey-like tree-climbing talents. I don't know about trees, but I'm sure Steve McNair could make me climb the walls!

JIM HARBAUGH

Sign: Capricorn
Born: December 23, 1963
Hometown: Toledo, Ohio
College: Michigan
Team: San Diego Chargers
Position: Quarterback
Number: 4
Draft Date: 1987
Draft Team: Chicago Bears

Jim Harbaugh is my veteran pick. A girl can always use a man with experience and good hands. Jim has had twelve seasons in the NFL and has been in the playoffs six times. He formed the Harbaugh Hill Foundation that helped distribute Colts tickets to underprivileged youths in Indianapolis. Charitable Jim also served as chairman for the Indiana Children's Miracle Network. Jim has spread his handsome grin on a few television programs, including *The Tonight Show* and *Saved by the Bell*.

FRANK SANDERS

Sign: Aquarius
Born: February 17, 1973
Hometown: Fort Lauderdale, Florida
College: Auburn
Team: Arizona Cardinals
Position: Wide receiver
Number: 81
Draft Date: 1995
Draft Team: Arizona Cardinals

Good looks, talent, and brains. Who could ask for anything more in Frank Sanders? He began his rookie year in 1995, and as soon as his feet hit the field, he began to play with the confidence and flair of a veteran player. Frank majored in psychology at Auburn. I'd lie down on a couch anytime for this guy!

EDGERRIN JAMES

Sign: Leo
Born: August 1, 1978
Hometown: Immokalee, Florida
College: Miami
Team: Indianapolis Colts
Position: Running back
Number: 32
Draft date:1999
Draft Team: Indianapolis Colts

Yes, Edgerrin James is a great player (he is even on Chuck's list), but more importantly he is single. Single and a stud. Single, a stud, and nice. He is a guest speaker for local schools for the DARE (Drug Abuse Resistance Education) program. He established the Edgerrin James Foundation, which is designed to promote charitable activities for underprivileged children and families to help improve their quality of life in their respective communities. He also donated $250,000 to the University of Miami's athletic department. Edgerrin lives in Indianapolis, Indiana. Did I mention he was single? Pack the car, I hear Indianapolis is beautiful this time of year.

COREY FULLER

Sign: Taurus
Born: May 1, 1971
Hometown: Tallahassee, Florida
College: Florida State
Team: Cleveland Browns
Position: Defensive back
Number: 24
Draft Date: 1995
Draft Team: Minnesota Vikings

This guy is a big cutie. With such smooth, high cheekbones and such a strong jawline, he looks as if an artist just carved him from stone. In college, Corey was one of eleven recipients of the College Football Association's "Good Works Team" award, given to recognize community involvement. Corey earned a degree in criminology and child development. Hey, if he feels like developing a child, I'm sure we could help him out.

MIKE HOLLIS

Sign: Gemini
Born: May 22, 1972
Hometown: Kellog, Idaho
College: Idaho
Team: Jacksonville Jaguars
Position: Kicker
Number: 1
Draft Date: Free agent
Draft Team: Free agent

Mike is my kicker pick... er. Kickers may not get enough respect around the league, but I'll treat him right. Mike is a baby-faced sweetie whose motto is "Never take anything for granted." He initiated the Kicks for Kids program in 1998 to benefit the American Cancer Society. He appeared in a public service safety message for the Wolfson Children's Hospital and supports activities that benefit the Jacksonville Children's Commission. Mike enjoys seafood and his favorite band is U2.

CHAD COTA

Sign: Leo
Born: August 13, 1971
Hometown: Ashland, Oregon
College: Oregon
Team: Indianapolis Colts
Position: Defensive back
Number: 37
Draft Date: 1995
Draft Team: Carolina Panthers

Chad Cota has got the best set of baby blues in the NFL. One look from those eyes and you will melt. Chad earned a degree in sociology at Oregon. Unfortunately, he lives in Charlotte with his wife, Christina. You can look, just don't touch!

MARK FIELDS

Sign: Scorpio
Born: November 9, 1972
Hometown: Los Angeles, California
College: Washington State
Team: New Orleans Saints
Position: Linebacker
Number: 55
Draft Date: 1995
Draft Team: New Orleans Saints

Mark Fields has the biggest, friendliest grin in the NFL. That grin just makes me want to chase him around the field and pinch him! This 6' 2", 244-pound giant looks like a lot of fun. I'd love to go out for a beer with this guy. Hey, Mark. I'm in the book. Marky Fun-boy donates to A Children's Wish of Greater New Orleans for every tackle and sack he makes. Coincidentally, Mark is single, at least until I get my paws on him. I'm gonna pinch him until he squeals like a little schoolgirl!

CHUCK'S LIST: LEGENDS IN THE MAKING

Okay, forget Teena's little list of top ten hot-panted hotties, and let's get down to business. If you're going to watch some football, you have to know who to watch for the right reasons—because they have all the right moves… uh… because they're powerful hunks of muscle… uh… because they can take a beating and come back for more… uh… okay, screw it, Teena can turn anything I say into some kind of sex thing so I'll just tell you the ten players to watch this year. I went a little heavy on the offense just because if you're a new fan, these are the names you'll keep hearing and these are the guys who make the fireworks (oh, crap, cue Teena with the sex joke). There are many fine centers, guards, ends, safeties, and kickers who didn't make the list, and I apologize to all of them, except the kickers.

JUNIOR SEAU: SCARY SPEED AND STRENGTH

Team: San Diego Chargers
Position: Outside linebacker
Number: 55
Draft Date: 1990
Draft Team: San Diego Chargers

I'd rather wear a chicken-wing suit into a Weight Watchers convention than try to sneak past Junior with a football in my hands. The San Diego Chargers linebacker is fast, strong, and tough. He will pursue, tackle, and stomp anyone and is equally capable of knocking the goo out of the quarterback, intercepting a pass, or chasing down a receiver and making him wish he had just dropped the ball. Seau (pronounced "Say ow!") has been called rare, special, and one of those players who can change a game and pump up everyone around him.

RAY LEWIS: JUST PLAIN SCARY

Team: Baltimore Ravens
Position: Linebacker
Number: 52
Draft Date: 1996
Draft Team: Baltimore Ravens

He was the NFL's defensive player of the year in 2000 and led what may be the best-ever defense to the Super Bowl title. He has added Super Bowl MVP to his list of accomplishments after a turbulent year, including being charged with murder following a Super Bowl party on January 31, 2000. But I don't want to go down that road. Like I said, Ray's scary.

PEYTON MANNING: FUTURE GREATNESS ARRIVES

Team: Indianapolis Colts
Position: Quarterback
Number: 18
Draft Date: 1998
Draft Team: Indianapolis Colts

It didn't take long for this kid to get the hang of the big time. In just a few years, Peyton's place as one of the game's top passers is secured, and he's not even close to hitting his prime yet. Peyton is surrounded by greatness in receiver Marvin Harrison, one of the game's best. He also has the strong runner Edgerrin James to take some pressure off his arm. Peyton is smart, has an accurate arm, and can go deep if the need arises. The Colts will be a good team for a long time, thanks to Peyton.

KURT WARNER: CLEANUP IN AISLE THREE
Team: St. Louis Rams
Position: Quarterback
Number: 13
Draft Date: Free agent
Draft Team: Free agent (signed with Rams in 1997)

We all know the story. One day the guy's bagging Froot Loops at the local Piggly Wiggly, and the next he's taking home a shopping cart full of NFL awards. He's a Super Bowl champ and an MVP. Not bad for a guy who was brought in as a backup. Now the question is, can Kurt Warner continue, or was his stellar 1999 season a fluke? He was injured for much of the 2000 season, so only time will tell. Kurt probably isn't the most skilled passer, but he has great receivers and backs to help him out. He doesn't have a cannon arm, but he's accurate, cool, and seems to be able to slide those passes in where his receivers can grab them.

TERRELL DAVIS: REBUILT BIGGER, STRONGER, FASTER
Team: Denver Broncos
Position: Running back
Number: 30
Draft Date: 1995
Draft Team: Denver Broncos

Terrell, who was partly responsible for John Elway finally winning a Super Bowl or two, was badly hurt in 1999, and his recovery and longevity are in question. He tore up his knee and may never be the same again, but don't count him out. Hell, this is the new millennium. If we can't do some Bionic Man stuff with Davis's knee, then we've failed as a civilization. The guy's good, strong, and works hard. He's barely tasted success, and he'll want to play again and be the best again. Terrell is a wild runner and can bounce off tacklers like a pinball. He has good speed in the open field, too.

EDDIE GEORGE: LAST NAME FIRST

Team: Tennessee Titans
Position: Running back
Number: 27
Draft Date: 1996
Draft Team: Houston Oilers

I normally don't trust guys with two first names, but I had to include Eddie because he's huge. At 6' 3" and 230 pounds, Eddie does a pretty good imitation of a bowling ball when he hits the line of scrimmage. He's wily, too, and can sit back and wait for a seam to develop or for someone to throw a key block that will spring him loose. And he makes the list because, as you'll see, there is an inordinate number of great football players with a first name for a last name. I couldn't exclude them all.

MARSHALL FAULK: DANCER AND PRANCER

Team: St. Louis Rams
Position: Running back
Number: 28
Draft Date: 1994
Draft Team: Indianapolis Colts

Marshall (I don't give a) Faulk is probably the best all-around offensive threat in the game. He's kind of wimpy when blocking and smashing, but he's got soft hands and he's quick enough to stay away from the mucky mucks in the pit. Marshall's a dancer who would rather bounce around looking for a big break than slam through the line for a few kidney-shredding yards. And he's the favorite last resort for quarterback Kurt Warner. When pass rushers threaten to turn Kurt into schnitzel, there's always Marshall to take a quick pass and turn it into a big play.

Snowboarding

EDGERRIN JAMES: NICKNAME IN WAITING
Team: Indianapolis Colts
Position: Running back
Number: 32
Draft Date: 1999
Draft Team: Indianapolis Colts

This guy makes the list just for his name. Edgerrin. How cool is that? His buddies Dave and Bubba can just call him "The Edge" for short. Edge is but a pup, but he's already left his mark, rushing for more than 1,500 yards in his rookie season. The kid can run; he's a natural simply because he's surefooted and tough to knock down. He's also powerful and is valuable in short-yardage situations. But he can also catch, and is sure-handed and reliable as a receiver. On top of all that, Teena says he is a stud.

ISAAC BRUCE: MR. STICKY HANDS
Team: St. Louis Rams
Position: Wide receiver
Number: 80
Draft Date: 1994
Draft Team: Los Angeles Rams

Say you have this football, right, and you want to get rid of it, okay? Well, if you need to just fling it out there and hope someone will catch it, Isaac is your guy. Another of these two first-name guys that I so distrust, Isaac Bruce can pluck footballs out of Nowhere Land. He also seems to be telepathically linked with QB Kurt Warner, making this duo dynamic.

CRIS CARTER: OLD TEACHER STILL HAS SOME TRICKS
Team: Minnesota Vikings
Position: Wide Receiver
Number: 80
Draft Date: 1987
Draft Team: Philadelphia Eagles

Not quite grizzled, but old nonetheless, Carter is tough, smart, and probably has the best hands in the game. He's acrobatic, quick, and can fake his coverage out, then blow by—leaving defenders wondering how bad a butt-chewing they can expect when they get to the bench. Carter is also a mentor and has taken troubled young receiver Randy Moss under his wing. Which brings us to…

RANDY MOSS: DO AS I SAY, GRASSHOPPER
Team: Minnesota Vikings
Position: Wide receiver
Number: 84
Draft Date: 1998
Draft Team: Minnesota Vikings

Completing the receiving duo that could make even me look good as a QB, Moss has blossomed in a short time to become one of the best at his job of catching footballs. Moss is a natural talent and he can jump like a kangaroo rat with a hot foot. If he's dedicated, he could be one of the best ever.

LARRY ALLEN: EARTH-SHATTERING LINEMAN
Team: Dallas Cowboys
Position: Guard
Number: 73
Draft Date: 1994
Draft Team: Dallas Cowboys

Since they are such unsung heroes, I had to sneak at least one big offensive lineman into this list. And if you're only going to take one workhorse, a 325-pound guy named Larry can't be a bad choice. As a guard, Larry's job is to either protect his quarterback or blow open some holes for his running backs. When you're strong, quick, and agile like Larry, you're going to create some pretty major holes. He is the best offensive lineman in the league and has five straight Pro Bowl selections to prove it.

WARREN SAPP: THE MAN WHO MOVES MOUNTAINS
Team: Tampa Bay Buccaneers
Position: Defensive tackle
Number: 99
Draft Date: 1995
Draft Team: Tampa Bay Buccaneers

When doing battle with the Larry Allens of the world, you better come big or stay home. If I'm a defensive coordinator, I'm bringing in Warren Sapp. He's another quick, agile 300-pounder who can be impossible to block. If you're playing against him, it can feel like he's everywhere, and when he's on, he makes it a long day for the offensive line. Sapp also has some pretty cool Bo Derek-esque cornrows going on and says he wants to be the first Hall of Famer with braids. His vanity plates read QBKILLR. That he is.

DEION SANDERS: PRIME-TIME PLAYER

Team: Washington Redskins
Position: Cornerback
Number: 21
Draft Date: 1989
Draft Team: Atlanta Falcons

Grudgingly, Deion makes the list, and grudgingly, I admit he's an all-time great at pass coverage. I don't know why he bugs me, but he does. It's not even the arrogance, the dancing, the showboating, or the damn hairnet he wears. It's just Deion. He might be a little too good for his own good. Then again, if I could do what he does, I'd do a little dance, too. But I still wouldn't wear a do rag to work. All that aside, Deion changes games. He is so quick, so good, so dominating that he pretty much takes a team's best wide receiver out of the game plan. He also scares the hell out of quarterbacks and offensive coaches, forcing them to change their game plans. Deion is also an offensive threat and could return a punt for six points any time. And he likes to try to be one of those old-time two-way players, going in as a wide receiver sometimes. Pound for pound, Deion "Prime Time" Sanders is—I hate to say it—the man.

9

Who are those bimbos on the sidelines?

THE CULTURE OF CHEERLEADERS

Did you ever want to be a cheerleader? Me neither.

You do have to admit that there is something strangely fascinating about them. Everyone likes to look at the cheerleaders. Maybe it is their perfectly straight teeth, their long flowing hair, their young tight butts, or those perky boobs. Whatever it is, cheerleaders appear to be the pinnacle of physical beauty and health. As regular women, we have to make a decision about cheerleaders: we can admire them for their surface beauty (a healthy, secure attitude); we can think that they are stupid to rely on their looks (a morally superior attitude, not quite as healthy as the first); or we can make fun of them. I have decided on the last option. If you are one of those obsessively moral, politically correct people, then you'd better skip directly to the next chapter.

The Evolution of the Bouncing Boobs

Now that we've gotten rid of the squares, let's continue. When I began my football quest, I thought that it was a totally macho game. The bouncing bimbos in the tiny tops didn't help the game's appearance. When I asked one of my football friends about the importance of cheerleaders in football, he brushed me off with the following comment:

"Teena, no one even looks at the cheerleaders. Well, you may catch a glance of them, but the real action is on the field. That is what all fans pay attention to, not the cheerleaders." Does he really think that I'm that stupid?

Chuck: Aw, come on. I didn't think you were stupid. It's true I hardly even notice the cheerleaders.

Who can we thank for the invention of cheerleading? Surprise, it's a man. The man to thank is not only a lunkhead but an educated lunkhead. In the 1880s, on the Princeton campus, a chant could be heard resonating from the football field. It went like this: "Ray, ray, ray! Tiger, tiger, tiger! Sis, sis, sis! Boom, boom, boom! Aaaaah! Princeton, Princeton, Princeton!" Yes, it may have sounded like garbled gibberish, but this was officially the first cheer known to football. In 1884, a graduate from Princeton, Thomas Peebles (the lunkhead in question), took that mangled mouthful to the University of Minnesota, where he was an undergraduate. It was here that cheerleading took root. Just in case you're ever on *Jeopardy*, here is a brief history of cheerleading:

1870s: The first pep club was established at Princeton.

1880s: The famous yell was yelled.

1890s: Organized cheerleading was set up at the University of Minnesota, and the first official fight song was born.

1900s: The megaphone became popular (like they weren't annoying enough).

1910: The first homecoming was held at the University of Illinois.

1920s: Women began cheerleading. Yup, that's right, before the 1920s, men were the only ones bouncing around. Finally, someone told them that they looked stupid in those skirts.

1930s: Paper pom-poms were used.

1940s: The American Cheerleaders Association was formed, the first national organization for cheerleaders.

1950s: College campuses began teaching "fundamental cheerleading skills." Classes like "Pushup Bras 101" were offered and "Booty-Shaking" skills were cultivated.

1960s: Vinyl pom-poms were invented. Now girls around the nation could go back to using tissue paper for what it was originally intended for—stuffing their bras.

1970s: The first nationwide broadcast of the National Collegiate Cheerleading Championships took place on CBS in the spring of 1978. Not a lawn was mowed that day, and couches across the nation moaned under the stress.

Today: Present cheerleaders are trying to update their ditzy image by getting involved in community service projects (posing for *Playboy*).

Famous Cheerleaders: I Was Once a Cheerleader, But I'm Feeling Much Better Now

There are a few famous cheerleaders that your football guy may not know about. We expect women such as Cheryl Ladd to be a cheerleader, but how about President Dwight D. Eisenhower?

> **Chuck:**
> Aw, come on, stop that! You are wrecking a national icon!

Or how about Jimmy Stewart?

> **Chuck:**
> Okay, that is going too far. I'm going to burn that list!

It seems that football fans love their cheerleaders as much as their players. It appears that the bubbling bimbos play an important role in the game after all. For the truth, I consulted many football cultural media to see what fans say about the importance of the vivacious vixens. I found many features such as "Cheerleader of the Day." I also went on-line, and at each of the team sites I found more of the same. And I could hardly open a football magazine without a pair of young boobs jumping out at me like an X-rated pop-up book. So, let's face the truth about cheerleaders. They are important, and they are noticed.

> **Chuck:**
> Please don't tell my wife. I beg you. It took me three years to convince her that the "Raiderettes" were just small football players.

booty

How to Shake That Thang

Now that you know the role cheerleaders play in the game of football, maybe you would like to drop that briefcase and pick up a pair of pom-poms. Before you do, you may want to consider what it takes to be a successful cheerleader. I have spent many hours researching the skills you need to become one of these football goddesses. I have read countless cheerleaders' bios, and believe me, every one of them read like a Miss America interview.

For example: "Amber is a two-year veteran of the squad. She is a graduate of Ruth Anne's College of High Hair and Tight Pants, and she is currently pursuing a career in modeling. When Amber is not cheering, she can be found brushing her hair, volunteering at the local Sick Children's hospital, and patting kittens. One day Amber hopes to invent world peace."

Aside from dazed eyes, a cheerleader must have a few other attributes. She does have to be athletic because no one wants to see a saggy-butt Raiderette. She must also be a sports fan because, if you don't know what a touchdown is, you don't know when to bounce your pom-poms. A good cheerleader must be able to stop moving to pose for calendar photo shoots. A background in dance is very helpful to a would-be cheerleader, but the ability to bounce incessantly is sometimes close enough. A cheerleader must be adept at bonding with other rattlebrained chicks who spend more time on their nails than reading. Above all, a cheerleader must be perky. And twenty years old.

Still interested in the job? Still believe that you are so perky you make Kathie Lee look like Eeyore? Then I will tell you how to become a cheerleader. You must begin dance class at the age of two; you must dedicate your whole life to cultivating a perfect, healthy body; and you must spend years studying under great cheerleading gurus. No, I'm just joking. All you need to do is get yourself some fake knockers and try out. You and a few hundred other nitwits will be exposed to a series of elimination tryouts. When the asinine group is weeded out to the chosen few, you will have to commit to practice three times a week plus game day. On the days that you do not practice, you will be working out on your own because you know the rule: "Saggy one day, sacked the next." A cheerleader can expect to do lots of charity work with squat for pay, although the job does reward you with the respect and admiration of your peers. Ooops, no, that's a doctor. Your peers will think that you are an airhead.

THE RIGHT MOVES

Still want to be a cheerleader? Didn't think so, but here are directions to a few moves just in case you want to pretend to be one. You know, make "Brett Favre and the Hot Cheerleader" night authentic.

Kick Line: You know this one. It is when you stand with your arms linked around the other dimwits on your squad and kick really high. This looks like group vertical splits and inspires all sorts of sexy harem fantasies in football guys.

Toe-Touch Jump: This move is when you jump up high and fling your arms and legs out parallel to each other, doing the splits in midair. It is also recommended that you lean forward slightly in this move to give the cameras a nice boob shot. I don't know what kind of fantasies this one inspires, but I'm sure that they are weird.

Toss in Hollow Position: This move is when two other banal bouncers chuck one girl up into the air. The chuckee remains in an "L" position until she lands. She either lands on her feet or is caught in a "cradle." Sometimes, she lands on her head. I don't know how this can happen, but you can bet that little bitch won't use your eyeliner again.

Double Lunge: This one is when you are bent over at the waist with your hands on your knees. It is sometimes used as a dance step (bouncing the boobs slightly) or as another girl braces herself on you to form a pyramid of chicks. This offers a chance for maximum cleavage exposure and inspires bizarre sexual fantasies of stackable concubines in sports fans.

"I Am the Best. I Am the Best. I Am the Best... "

I do have to admit that during my research into the cheerleading culture, I have come to like the cheers and chants. I have a theory that if only we could integrate cheers into our daily personal lives, the world would be an easier place. Imagine that you are getting ready to present a big proposal to a client. You walk into a packed room and everyone breaks into:

CLEAVAGE

> Here comes Teena
> She's so great
> Give the proposal
> We can't wait!
> Goooooo Teena!

I have consulted *The Official Cheerleader's Handbook* to provide you with authentic cheers to inspire you in your daily life.

> Break away
> Move ahead
> We're breakin' away
> Break away!

Useful on the highway for passing and diffuses road rage. It is impossible to flip someone the bird when you are singing this little ditty.

I like this one when you-know-who thinks the big game is more fun than hitting the sack with you:

> Score big
> Score more
> Score now
> S-C-O-R-E
> Score big
> Score more
> Score now!

This one is a good willpower booster. It is useful at times when you are feeling a bit weak, like at midnight when you hear that triple fudge cake calling from the kitchen, "Eat me. Eat me!" You can reply:

> Up with victory
> Down with defeat
> Super Teena
> Won't be beat!

Now you know all that is needed to become a cheerleader. I'm sure that there is some work involved, and I'm also sure that cheerleaders are nice girls. In fact, some of my closest friends are cheerleaders. Or they were my friends. Anyway, if you want to be a bouncing idiot, go ahead.

Did he just touch his butt?

Girls, there are some questions that you just don't want to ask unless you want to be tormented for the rest of your life by the condescending laughter of your football guy. This chapter will provide you with some of those answers and save you the echoing bellows of ridicule that I received when I asked.

Did He Just Touch His Butt?

I know, I know. The relationship between the center and the quarterback seems a bit, shall we say, personal. But, apparently, it is the job of the quarterback to get so close to the center.

Through my research, I have found a description of the quarterback's stance. The quarterback places his hands under the center's butt, with his thumbs touching each other and his fingers spread. The quarterback then lowers his hands below the center's rear end (in order to receive the ball cleanly). Sounds like he is getting ready to grab a big handful of tushie to me.

tushie

How Important Is the Quarterback, Really?

The quarterback is very important. Not only must he have amazing technical skills, but he must be able to make good decisions under pressure. He must be able to make his calls and change the plays without messing up, or he will hear from everyone. What would happen if the quarterback couldn't make the calls, if he lost his voice? Would the game be over, or would they work around it? Hey, Chuck, what happens?

Chuck:

Well, Teena, in September 1980, the San Francisco 49ers had to deal with this exact situation. Their quarterback, Steve DeBerg, had contracted laryngitis. After screaming through a victory over the New Orleans Saints, poor Steve didn't have much of a voice left during the following week of practice. Did the 49ers bench him? Heck no. They got special permission from the NFL to wire his helmet with a microphone so that his teammates could hear his cadence calls. It worked, and Steve led the 49ers to a victory over the Cardinals.

Why Do Some Players Wear a Loincloth Towel?

Players such as the quarterback who often throw the ball wear a loincloth towel. They need the towel to dry their hands; otherwise, their grip on the ball would be slippery. The NFL even regulates the towel; they can be only eight inches long and six inches wide, and must be tucked into the front waist of the pants.

Why Does the Quarterback Lift His Leg?

When working out of the "shotgun," with the quarterback lined up a few yards behind the center, it can be hard for the snapper to hear the "Hike!" call. So, just to make sure everyone's in sync, the quarterback

lifts his foot up, puts it back down, and everyone counts in their head. Then comes the snap. This technique is needed especially when playing on the road because the noise of the home fans makes it almost impossible to hear the quarterback.

What is That Black Stuff Under Their Eyes?

No, they did not forget to take off their mascara before the shower. These guys look like raccoons for a reason—the black smudge under the eyes absorbs bright sunlight and reduces the glare. Players either smear on this greasy substance (it comes in a tube that looks suspiciously like lipstick), or they use special pieces of black tape.

What Are Those Strips on Their Noses?

If your football guy snores like an asthmatic hippo, then this information could be helpful. Those peel-and-stick strips you see some players wearing help them breathe and, since their invention, have been used to help prevent snoring. You can run to the drugstore right now and thank sports technology for a restful night's sleep.

What the Hell Am I Supposed to Be Looking At?

For many reasons, I recommend watching the quarterback. He's tall and muscular, and knows where to find the action. And if he doesn't, the action will find him. Once you become a professional armchair quarterback, you'll be able to pick up the subtleties of the position, and you'll be able to tell whether your guy is on top of his game. Watch how fast he takes the snap and drops back to throw. Does he look calm? Is he looking all over the field for an open receiver? Is he holding the ball high for a quick release? These are all good things to look for and point out to your buddies. Here's what you say: "Man, McNair looks good today. Look how quick he's dropping into the pocket. Much better than last week." It's a subtle toss-off line that will showcase your deep knowledge of the game.

When Should I Go for a Tinkle?

Never, say hardcore fans. But, then, even hardcore fans need to find time to grab another brew. So, when should you make a break for the loo? During a commercial, duh? Or halftime is good. Otherwise, right after a touchdown isn't a bad time since the point after conversion kick is almost always a given. Never go on third down, or you'll look like a rookie.

When Does the Game Get Exciting?

Things start to heat up whenever the offense gets in the "red zone." The red zone is within twenty yards of the end zone; it's called this because the defense is on red alert since a score is imminent. Defenses try to form a wall; offenses pull out all their tricks or just use all their strength and power to bust the ball over the goal line. The fans go crazy. The tension mounts. Don't go for nachos now. Big plays can happen anytime. That's the beauty of football. A team will throw a long bomb out of nowhere, when you aren't expecting it. They'll try an onside kick on the opening kickoff. They'll fake a punt, fake a field goal, fumble, throw an interception. Every time the ball is snapped, something good could happen—unless you cheer for a team whose name rhymes with "Mincinnati Mengals."

What the Heck Do They Feed Those Boys to Make Them So Big?

Steroids. At least, that used to be the answer until the NFL began to crack down on drug use. Now, I think they just eat a lot. Former Cowboys defensive end Daniel Stubbs used to come to practice every day with a monster sandwich made of two fried eggs, sausage, bacon, and cheese on Texas toast. TV analyst John Madden named it an "All-Madden Sandwich" because when he tried to get it analyzed at a clinic, the doctor wouldn't even touch it. He picked it up with tongs and said it was the most fat and cholesterol-loaded thing he'd ever seen.

Generally, a player's diet is very important, and if he strays from it he could be in big trouble. Ask Seattle Seahawks Rick Mirer, Corez Kennedy, and Eugene Robinson what happens if you stray from your prescribed diet. All three players were fined $1,000 by their coach, Dennis Erikson, for eating hot dogs on the sidelines during a game.

Eddie Lebaron, the Dallas Cowboys' quarterback in the 1960s, was once overheard ordering steak at a team meal: "Don't bother to cook mine. Just turn the bull loose, and I'll rip a hunk off as he goes by." Yipes!

The three daily steak and potato meals for football players ended with bell-bottoms and disco. Players these days focus on complex carbohydrates—lots of pasta, rice, and grains—and tons of veggies and fruit, with a small bit of lean meat or fish. They also drink a lot of water, fruit juice, and specially engineered sports drinks. But don't think that changing your football guy's diet will turn him into the Greek-godlike specimens that we see playing football. It isn't food alone that grows such giants.

Are Players Really That Tough?

With all the training these boys do, they are very, very strong. We just need to look to receiver Gerald Riggs of the Washington Redskins for proof. During practice in 1989, Riggs was running for a pass and ended up colliding with a pickup truck parked near the sidelines. Gerald was

completely unhurt; the pickup wasn't so lucky. Gerald caused $1,370 worth of damage to the truck, including a severely dented door and broken window.

Chicago Bears fullback Bronko Nagurski can also help illustrate this point. During a game, Bronko broke into the clear and ran to the end zone—with such force that he ran right into a mounted policeman and sent the officer and his horse ass over teakettle.

The Stereotype is That Football Players Are Lunkheads. Are They Really That Dumb?

I would never be one to continue such silly stereotypes, so we will let the words of Dallas Cowboys all-time great running back Duane Thomas illustrate the point. Duane responded to someone questioning his own I.Q. by replying, "Sure, I got one. It's a perfect 20/20."

Or maybe we will let Joe Theismann, former star quarterback for the Washington Redskins, defend the football players. In 1993, Joe said, "The word genius isn't applicable in football. A genius is a guy like Norman Einstein."

What Do Players Do to Relieve Stress?

We all know the best way to relieve stress—nudge, nudge, wink, wink. And if any NFL players are having trouble taking care of that, I will do my football fan's duty and help them out. Anything for the game.

That aside, players often find creative ways to deal with the frustration of losing a game. Jack "Hacksaw" Reynolds is a great example of bizarre ingenuity. Jack was a linebacker with the Los Angeles Rams and the San Francisco 49ers from 1970 to 1984. He got his choppy nickname while he was in college. Reynolds was really pissed off that his team had just taken a beating in the previous game. To relax, he went for a long walk to a serene bluff overlooking a river. On the bluff was an old 1950s Chevrolet with no motor. Jack was inspired. He ran out to the local hardware store for supplies and then went to work. Eight hours and fourteen hacksaw blades later, Jack had hand-sawed the car in half and given himself a new nickname.

How Much Do These Guys Get Paid? And What Is a "Salary Cap"?

The first professional football player in recorded history was John Braillier, who was paid a whopping ten bucks for his efforts in 1895. Some claim that Walter "Pudge" Heffelfinger from Yale was the first, receiving $500 for a game. Before the first national professional football league was established in 1920, players' salaries ranged from $50 to $250 and college players assumed aliases so that they could play professionally on Sunday afternoons. Either way, none of those salaries can compare with what today's players earn.

The average pay for an NFL player has increased dramatically in the past ten years. In 1988, the average NFL player's salary was US$250,000; now, a star quarterback can be paid as much as $12 million. At the bottom of the ladder, a first-year player could earn around $150,000, which isn't bad for a starting wage.

I'm sure you've heard your football guy yack about salary caps. Simply put, salaries depend on how much the team makes. The cap is based on players getting 63 percent of the team's revenue, including product sales, concessions, parking, ticket sales, and television contracts. This was a negotiated labor settlement between the NFL owners and the players' association designed to put teams on an equal footing when it comes to free agents and draft picks.

There are a lot more details in explaining the fine points of the salary cap (I'm sure you've already heard some from your guy), but that is basically it. The most common complaint is that sometimes teams lose their stars because of salary cap restrictions (I'm sure you've heard that lament, too).

They Play in Rain, Sleet, and Snow. Will Anything Stop This Game?

They may play through any weather dropping from the sky, but they will stop if it is pigeon droppings landing on their heads. The Buffalo Bills, under the coaching of Lou Saban, had to reschedule practice because of a pigeon invasion. On the first day of practice, the Bills discovered the smelly little poop bombers all over their field and began chasing them from end zone to end zone. This only upset the birds and caused them to become even faster poopers. Practice had to be canceled, and coach Saban called the police to take care of the problem. When the team showed up the next day, the field was surrounded by police sharpshooters picking off the birds. The shooting made the players too nervous to play, so practice was canceled again. This time, Saban called the health department, which spread poisoned seed all over the field. That would fix the pesky poop problem. The following day, practice had to be canceled again. The birds had their final revenge when they all died on the football field, covering it with dead birdie carcasses.

This Is a Terribly Rough Game. Has Anyone Ever Died Playing?

Sometimes it is terrifying to watch the bodies fly through the air, somersaulting and crashing. It looks like someone could die at any minute. The last player to die from an injury during play was Howard Glenn of the New York Titans in 1960, from a broken neck.

What Is Arena Football?

Arena football is an indoor, faster version of football played in an arena built for basketball or hockey. Its rules are a little different from the NFL's. Arena football is played with only eight players on the field at one time (as opposed to the NFL's eleven), and six of those eight players play on both the offensive and defensive lines for the team. The field, of course, is much smaller than NFL fields. Arena football does not allow blitzing, and the defensive team is only allowed to rush the quarterback with four players. Another difference is that there is no punting in this game. With all kickoffs and missed field goals, the returner retrieves the ball after it has deflected off the netting in the end zone.

Arena football is a faster-paced, more offensive-oriented game. I tried watching it before I completely understood NFL rules and almost lost my mind. I recommend understanding the NFL game before tackling the arena game. The good thing is that the arena season begins in May, so you can watch football all summer.

Why Is the Field Called the Gridiron, and How Do They Put the Marks on It?

Early football fields were drawn with a crosshatch grid of lines to help officials, making it look like a gridiron. Apparently, the name stuck. The markings are put on the field with paint or marking chalk. They even use paint to put the lines on the grass. Now, there's a good idea. No more listening to the neighbors complain about the state of the lawn, just get some NFL field paint and have the coolest lawn in the neighborhood.

Are Women Allowed in the Locker Rooms?

They sure are! Not only can we go mingle with sweaty—or freshly showered—naked men, it's our constitutional right. A federal judge decreed this in 1978 after *Sports Illustrated* writer Melissa Ludke was denied access to the New York Yankees' locker room during the 1977 World Series.

Women actually first started heading to the showers during World War II, when there was a shortage of male reporters. But even after the 1978 court decision, women have struggled for respect and acceptance in this traditionally male domain. In 1984, reporter Cathy Henkel was ridiculed and yelled at by the Stanford Cardinals football team when she entered their locker room for some postgame interviews. She was escorted out while male reporters were allowed to stay.

Other lowlights in the women-in-the-locker-room saga include a baseball player sending a female sportswriter a rat in a gift box. Then there was the case of Lisa Olson, a *Boston Herald* writer, who ran into a bunch of cretins in the New England Patriots' locker room. They thought it would be funny to show off their dangly bits to her and taunted her with lewd comments. Lisa sued, and the team was ordered to provide instructional material to players on how to deal with the media. Rule number one: don't show them your wieners. Three players were also fined. Unfortunately, bitter New England management and fans forced Olson to move on to another paper in another country.

Today's players seem to be more comfortable with women in their locker rooms, and while the situation is uncomfortable for both sides, they both treat it as business. Female reporters keep their eyes up and their questions short, and the players show them the same respect as they do male reporters. Some players have said they don't care if it's a man or woman, as long as they don't ask dumb questions.

Has a Woman Ever Played Professionally?

In 1970, Pat Palinkas became the first woman to play professional football. The Orlando Panthers of the Atlantic Coast League signed her to hold the ball for her placekicking specialist husband, Steve. In a hilarious turn of events, Pat's hubby was cut from the squad, and Pat remained with the team. Pat's career didn't last long. When she realized what a lame-o job she had, she began playing hooky. She was suspended when she skipped too many practices. A woman has yet to play in the NFL.

Chuck's Chin-Waggin': A woman may not have played in the NFL, but there have been plenty of men whose names sound like women's. Here is a list of the ten most girly football player names: June Jones, Margene Adkins, Gail Cogdill, Blenda Gay, Fair Hooker, Dolly King, Blanche Martin, Julie Rykovich, Faye Wilson, and Tillie Manton.

How Else Are Women Involved in the Game?

We can do whatever the hell we want in this game.

Georgia Frontierre owns the St. Louis Rams—winners of Super Bowl XXXIV. Amy Trask is CEO of the Oakland Raiders. Lesley Vissor and Pam Oliver are two high-profile commentators. Ellen Zavian is a powerful player agent. There are seven female vice presidents or vice chairpersons in the NFL, and we chicks hold five key financial positions. We work for the league as legal advisors and administrators; we also work in public and community relations.

If you want to play, we have a league of our own. The Women's Professional League is free of hairy, testosterone beasts and plays by the NFL rules. WPL teams include the Minnesota Vixens, Lake Michigan Minx, and Nashville Dream.

Why Is Football Called a "Game of Inches"?

Not having been in a real football locker room, I can't answer that. Over to you, Chuck.

Chuck:
Thanks, Teena. This whole "game of inches" thing seems misleading because, let's face it, a football field is huge, and the game seems to revolve around big things. Football is about picking up some big yards, and it's about big players who are better measured in tons than pounds. But it's a game of inches because that's often what a game comes down to. A few inches can separate a win from a loss, a Super Bowl champ from a chump. Look at the "Immaculate Reception," for example. A few inches, and Franco Harris wouldn't have snagged that ball, and Pittsburgh would have been bounced from the playoffs.

Chuck, calm down, you're spitting.

In the Super Bowl in 2000, the Tennessee Titans learned why it's called a game of inches when Titan Kevin Dyson was stopped just short of scoring the game-tying touchdown on the final play of the game. Okay, so he was three feet short, but that's only thirty-six inches! That's three times ten inches plus a few! Practically there! Almost got it!

What Was the "Immaculate Reception?"

We won't ask Chuck to explain this one, he might have a coronary. The Immaculate Reception will go down as one of the most amazing, breathtaking clutch plays in the history of sport. Former Oakland Raiders coach John Madden, in his book, *All Madden*, says that he still gets mad every time he thinks about it. He's mad because the play broke the back of his Raiders in the 1972 playoffs and may have cost them a trip to the Super Bowl. Here's how it went down. The Raiders were leading 7–6 with twenty seconds to go. The Steelers were pinned on their own forty-yard line on fourth and ten. The Raiders rushed quarterback Terry Bradshaw, forcing him to scramble and toss a desperation pass off to Frenchy Fuqua. The ball bounced off either Frenchy or charging Raiders safety Jack Tatum and floated right into the hands of a rushing Steeler, Franco Harris, who rumbled all the way into the end zone untouched. What has Madden fuming still is that at the time, according to NFL rules, if the ball bounced off Frenchy, his teammates weren't eligible to catch it. Today, that rule is gone, and it wouldn't have made a difference, but in 1972 it did. Madden says the referees didn't signal a touchdown right away, because nobody knew who the ball hit. When the decision went against him, Madden said it was the low point of his career.

What's the "All-Madden Team?"

The All-Madden Team is an unofficial sort of all-star team created by ex-coach-turned-broadcaster John Madden. He has a real thing for old-time football and tough-nosed players (Okay, it's not just their noses that are tough), so every year he names his favorites and inducts them onto the team. It's an honor for players to be chosen, and for some it's a more coveted selection than the Pro Bowl. To be selected, a player must be gritty and willing to get dirty, and Madden must have seen him play in person that year. Some of the all-time All-Madden players include Joe Montana (quarterback), Walter Payton (running back), Jerry

Rice (wide receiver), Howie Long (defensive end), Lawrence Taylor (linebacker), Ronnie Lott (defensive back), and Pat Summerall (kicker). Summerall is also Madden's broadcast partner.

Who's This Heisman Guy?

John Heisman is the football innovator who created the snap from center and added the words "hep" and "hike" to our vocabulary. He also legalized the forward pass and invented the scoreboard. The trophy for U.S. college football's best player is called the Heisman Trophy. Past winners include O.J. Simpson and Doug Flutie.

What Do They Mean by "Parity"?

League parity means there's not too much separating the good teams from the bad. In any year, almost any team could be a playoff contender. In 1999, the St. Louis Rams went from a 4–12 record in the previous year to 13–3 and a Super Bowl championship. When a team makes a turnaround like that, other teams and fans take note and hope for the same kind of "Cinderella season." In other words, no teams are runaway favorites, and no teams are down and out. Except those two teams in Ohio. They both suck, always.

What Is up with Those Nicknames?

Unlike some sports, where nicknames can be perplexing and, at times, wussyish, football is full of colorful handles. And when the game gets boring, you can always add life to the party by coming up with some good ones yourself. Sometimes even a whole team has a nickname. The Dallas Cowboys are "America's Team," or at least they were until they got into the drugs and the hookers. The Chicago Bears of 1941 were the "Monsters of the Midway." In Minnesota, a once-fearsome defense was known as the "Purple People Eaters," while in Pittsburgh, a dominant defense that led the Steelers to four Super Bowls became known as "The Steel Curtain." In Washington, the Redskins offensive line was once known as "The Hogs." In some cities, even the fans have nicknames. In Green Bay, fans are known as "Cheeseheads," and they even wear little cheese-shaped hats. In Cleveland, fans call themselves the "Dawgs," and the bleachers are "The Dawg Pound." They've even been known to chuck biscuits at opposing players and, by the end of a long, beer-filled Sunday, to urinate on fire hydrants, lampposts, passed-out buddies…

Here are some of my all-time favorite football nicknames.

Charles "Red" Grange: "The Galloping Ghost"
Walter Payton: "Sweetness"
Jevon Kearse: "The Freak"
"Slingin'" Sammy Baugh
Reggie White: "The Minister of Defense"
William "The Refrigerator" Perry
Kenny "The Snake" Stabler
"Broadway" Joe Namath
"Mean" Joe Greene
"Iron" Mike Ditka
Dick "Night Train" Lane
Deion Sanders: "Prime Time"
Jerome Bettis: "The Bus"

And some nicknames just don't work.

Lance Allworth: "Bambi"
Ron Jaworski: "Jaws"
Richard Crump: "Chubby Chicken" (he loved chicken and beer)
Carlton Gilchrist: "Cookie"
Austin Gonsoulin: "Goose"
Harry Jagade: "Chick"
John Kelly: "Shipwreck"
Verda Smith: "Vitamin"
Fred Thurston: "Fuzzy"
Byron White: "Whizzer"

Super Chuck's Scuttlebutt: First of all, Teena, I hate this title. Now that it is off my chest, I can continue.

Here is a bit of trivia to stump your guy. Ask him who "Broadway Joe" was. As we all know, Broadway Joe is most famously Joe Namath. But he wasn't the first Joe to have this nickname. Joe Pepitone played first base for the Yankees of the American League (1962–69). He was the original Broadway Joe. Namath got the name in 1965 when he joined the New York Jets.

There you go, girls, I've provided all the answers that I've got. If you've got any more questions, do what I do—call Chuck at home. Anytime… day or night… his number is in the book.

So, you think you're smart, do you?

Girlfriends, I bet you are so full of football knowledge that by this point you are ready to start spewing football facts to anyone that passes by. Well, it's time to finely hone that smarty-pants attitude. This chapter will provide you with trivia to impress your loved ones and, most importantly, show up that know-it-all football guy of yours.

Presidential Veto

Which American President threatened to declare football illegal? Can you imagine it—illegal to play football? What would we do on Sunday afternoons?

It was President Theodore Roosevelt, who was moved by mounting protests over the brutality of the game in 1906. One editorial writer had described football as "wasteful, wanton barbarity... not fit for humans to indulge in, or even witness." Pretty tough description, but this wasn't the game we know today. In those days, few penalties had been defined, there were no rules discouraging brutality, and there was little or no safety equipment. An average of fifteen to twenty players died each year as a result of injuries sustained on the football field in the early 1900s. No wonder the President was upset.

In late November 1906, Roosevelt called together representatives of Harvard, Yale, and Princeton to the White House. He warned them that if football didn't clean up its act, he would abolish it. The college leaders listened and later organized a collegiate rules body that eventually became the National Collegiate Athletic Association. The rules were changed, penalties were added, and excessive violence soon disappeared. The game evolved into the one we know and love now—all due to the threatening stance Teddy Roosevelt took.

Southern Savior

Football in the southern states also had a near-death experience. In 1897, the South's finest colleges met. The University of Virginia and the University of Georgia were headed for battle, and Georgia was counting on their golden boy, Richard Von Gammon. Within a few minutes of the opening of the second half, Von Gammon was hit hard. The pileup was so vicious that Von Gammon was taken off the field unconscious with a concussion. Before the game was over, Von Gammon was dead.

Von Gammon was one of the game's most popular players, and his death created turmoil. The Georgia team was quickly disbanded, and many other colleges got rid of their teams. Protests against the brutality of the game rose to a frenzy, and a bill to outlaw the game was swiftly passed by the Georgia state legislature and sent to the governor. Other states drew up their own bills against the game, and the future of football in the southern states looked bleak. Then a letter arrived on the desk of the Georgia governor's desk.

"Von's love for his college and his interest in all manly sports is well-known by his teammates and classmates. Grant me the right to request that my boy's death not be used to defeat the most cherished object in his life."

The letter was signed, "Yours most respectfully, Von Gammon's mother." Her message hit home, and the governor did not sign the bill. Other states also dropped their bills against the game, and football was saved.

Girly Coach

The famous coach Walter Camp got too sick to coach shortly before the beginning of the 1888 season. Who do you think he called on to replace him? I bet Mr. Football Know-It-All would tell you it was his assistant coach. Well, Mr. Know-It-All is wrong. Walter didn't call on his assis-

tant, he called his wife to the rescue of the team. You know all the crap you have to do for the big baby when *he's* sick, just imagine how poor Mrs. Camp felt. A whiny husband all night and a whiny football team all day. By the way, substituting for her hubby, she led the team to victory in almost all of its games.

Pass It to Me

In October 1959, Milt Plum of the Cleveland Browns was in a desperate situation in a game against the Chicago Cardinals. Milt decided to pass to the wide receiver on his left side, but a Cardinal defender got in the way. The Cardinal player blocked the pass, the ball then deflected off him and back into the hands of Milt Plum. Plum took this opportunity and ran with it. He ran for a twenty-yard gain and put himself in the record books with the longest pass completion to himself.

Marshall "Broken" Law

In 1964, the defensive end for the Minnesota Vikings, Jim Marshall, was making headlines first for his talent, then for making an ass of himself. In a game against the San Francisco 49ers, Jim picked up a fumble and ran the amazing sixty-two yards that brought him into the end zone to score what he thought was a touchdown for his team. To Jim's humiliation, he had not scored six points for the Vikings but instead a safety for the 49ers. Muddleheaded Marshall had become so disoriented during the play that he ran the wrong way—a feat that we will never let him live down.

Good Guido

Guido Merkens played defensive cornerback for the Houston Oilers in 1978. When the Oilers needed help on the receiving end, Guido switched to wide receiver. Upon his return to the Oilers in 1979, Guido became their quarterback. In one year, the man played three different positions for one team. A man who is the master of many positions? I could use a man like that.

Superman Jack of All Trades

Cal Hubbard didn't have to choose between football and baseball. Cal was a giant lineman for Green Bay, New York, and Pittsburgh and did his job so well that he was entered into the Pro Football Hall of Fame. Talented Cal was also entered into the Baseball Hall of Fame for his achievements as an umpire. If only there was a Couch Potato Hall of Fame and a Doritos Chompin' Hall of Fame, our guys could be two-time Hall of Famers, too.

Name-Droppers

A long time ago, there was a town with an ugly name. This town's name was so ugly that it was difficult to draw tourists to the area and get funds for the new hospital. The town was called Mauch Chunk (sounds like a groundhog puking, doesn't it?). Mauch Chunk (in fact, it's starting to make me a bit nauseous) residents decided that they would redefine themselves through an association with a truly American symbol of greatness—a football hero. The town chose Jim Thorpe, and Jim Thorpe, Pennsylvania, was born.

Olympic Giveaway

Jim Thorpe won two gold medals in the 1912 Olympic Games. Unfortunately, Jim failed to mention that he had played minor-league baseball in North Carolina and was later disqualified. His gold for the pentathlon and the one for the decathlon were yanked. Despite the efforts of Congress and other loud supporters, the medals were never returned. That is what you get for lying on your resume.

Medals That the Athletes Got to Keep

Jim is not alone in his gold medal Olympic talent. Here is a list of other football players who are Olympic gold champions:

James Jett (Raiders): 1992 relay
Sam Graddy (Broncos, Raiders): 1984 relay
Ron Brown (Rams, Raiders): 1984 relay
Johnny "Lam" Jones (Jets): 1976 relay
Gerald Tinker (Falcons, Packers): 1972 relay
Tommie Smith (Bengals): 1968 200 meters

There are more champions, but since we weren't even alive when they won their medals (right, wink), who cares?

Leave Me Alone

I know your football guy would do almost anything to become a sports hero. Everyone would like to be worshipped and adored by thousands of fans. Everyone except Pat O'Dea.

Pat was one of the first stars in football to become a national sports idol. Pat was raised in Australia and moved to the States to go to college. In 1896, Pat tried out for the University of Wisconsin football team. He landed a spot as the team's halfback and proved to be a rugged player who could endure the full sixty minutes of each game. Pat also earned fame as one of the best dropkickers and placement kickers in the history of the game. He was soon nicknamed the "Kangaroo" and once punted a football for a distance of 110 yards. Pat was attracting hordes of fans to each game and was being mobbed wherever he went. So did he use his fame to gain fortunes and easy babes? Nope, not Pat O'Dea. One day Pat simply disappeared into thin air. The nation was shocked, and wild rumors of murder and shallow graves began to circulate. Seventeen long years passed before Pat O'Dea was discovered living and working in a small town, practically unknown to his neighbors. Pat had assumed the name Charles Mitchell, but after having his true identity discovered, he had to return to Pat O'Dea for the rest of his life.

Defensive Songbird

Football stars don't just express themselves creatively through acting. Mike Reid, Pro Bowl defensive tackle for the Cincinnati Bengals, retired abruptly in 1974 at the height of his career. Why would he do such a thing? He left to pursue a career as a full-time pianist and songwriter.

Mike reached the pinnacle of his new career when he won a Grammy as the top country songwriter. He wrote songs for many artists, including Ronnie Milsap, Joe Cocker, Barbara Mandrell, and the Oak Ridge Boys.

Unfair Advantage

As a child, Erny Pinckert thought he had a strange sister. When his sister told him that she had a vision that he would grow up to be a famous football player, he just thought that it was another episode of the Strange Sister. Erny grew, went to college, was an all-American at USC, and then played for the Boston/Washington Redskins from 1932 to 1940. Erny Pinckert did grow up to be a famous football star. But what became of his strange sibling? She grew up to be Jeanne Dixon, the famous psychic.

Anybody Got a Better Offer?

He may be one of the greatest quarterbacks ever to play, but it almost didn't happen. Joe Montana was offered a full scholarship to North Carolina State to play basketball upon his high school graduation. He had planned to accept until Notre Dame offered him a football scholarship.

Hey, What a Gyp

Joe Montana may have made it to Notre Dame to play football, but his potential was not immediately recognized. In his freshman year, he was the seventh-string signal caller.

Payback Is a Bitch

Montana soon proved his worth to Notre Dame. In 1975, late in the fourth quarter of a game against North Carolina, the score was 14–6, and things looked very bleak to everyone. Everyone except Joe. He led his team to a touchdown in five plays and then threw for a two-point conversion to tie the score. The next time he was on the field, he tossed an eighty-yard touchdown pass. Notre Dame won because Joe Montana helped his team score two touchdowns and a two-point conversion, all in the span of one minute and two seconds. I guess that's what you get for offering Joe Montana a scholarship for basketball.

Super Score

Who holds the record for the most points scored in a single game? Ernie Nevers of the Chicago Cardinals kicked the Chicago Bears, furry little butts when he scored six touchdowns and converted four extra points, totaling forty points in a game played in November 1929.

Born to Play

Which football player had the best football name? The 1953 Chicago Bears had a quarterback named Willie Thrower on their roster.

Most Famous Name

Who had the most famous name in football history? Let your guy sweat over this one because it wasn't a football name. When the Pittsburgh Steelers signed this player, they did a double take. The former Notre Dame player's name was William Shakespeare.

Poe Preference

Notre Dame may have preferred Shakespeare, but Princeton University has always been fond of Edgar Allan Poe. Six descendants of the famous American writer have played varsity on Princeton's gridiron.

A Rose by Any Other Name

"Not-so-nice" Joe Green doesn't exactly have the same ring to it. "Mean" Joe Green got his name when he played for the Pittsburgh Steelers in the early 1970s. Joe was stalking New York Giants player Fran Tarkenton. The giant, 270-pound Green tackled Tarkenton and planted him into the field surface. Tarkenton had already released the ball and Joe was called for roughing the passer. From that moment on, Charles Edward Green was known as "Mean Joe."

Grand Old Geezer

Ask Mr. Smarty-Pants if he knows who the "Grand Old Man of Football" is. Or ask him if he knows the only man who is immortalized in the Hall of Fame as a player and coach.

The "Grand Old Man of Football" was Amos Alonzo Stagg, who lived to be 103 years old before his death in 1965. Amos played football at Yale and was selected on the very first all-American team in 1889 by Walter Camp. Amos then began his coaching career in a YMCA training school called Springfield College. In 1892, he began coaching at the University of Chicago and remained there for forty years. And then did Amos retire? No way. In 1933, when the university made him a professor emeritus and retired him with a pension, the proud old geezer turned down the money: "I could not and would not accept a job without work. I am fit, able, and willing to continue as a football coach. I refuse to be idle and a nuisance."

At the ripe old age of seventy, Stagg went west to become the coach of College of the Pacific (a tiny college). He remained there for fourteen more seasons and was so successful that he was voted best football coach of the year by all the football coaches in the land. Did the amazing Amos retire then? No way. When the college offered him retirement, he once again turned it down. He then returned east to join his son, who was the coach at Susquehanna College in Pennsylvania. For the next six years, Stagg senior was on the field coaching the team's offense. In 1951, his team was undefeated, and Amos Alonzo Stagg finally retired at the age of ninety. In his long career, Amos was credited for many firsts: he invented the tackling dummy, he was the first to use the huddle, and he was the first to number the players' uniforms. And he was entered into the Hall of Fame as a player and coach.

Longest Boot

The score was 17–16, the year was 1970. With only eleven seconds left to play, the Detroit Lions looked like they would take the game over the New Orleans Saints. The Saints needed an impossible field goal to change the score. On to the field trotted their kicker, Tom Dempsey. The ball was snapped, and Dempsey kicked it. It sailed through the air for an astounding sixty-three yards to win the contest. What makes this NFL record even more astounding is that Tom Dempsey was born missing his right hand and part of his right foot—the record-setting kicking foot.

Biggest Losers

Early in the 1940 season, the Washington Redskins and the Chicago Bears met for a game. After this early game, the Redskins commented publicly that the Bears were a "first-half club" and that they would easily fold in the last two quarters of a game. Have you ever seen an angry bear? These guys were on fire. They filled their heads with as many plays from the Washington playbook as possible. They were out for revenge.

When the two teams next met, during a championship game, the Bears came out growling. In the second half, the official had to actually ask Chicago to stop kicking extra points because they were running out of balls. The game ended 73–0, proof of what will happen if you tangle with an angry bear.

Biggest Comeback

The San Francisco 49ers were trailing the New Orleans Saints by a pathetic score of 35–7 at halftime in a game on December 7, 1980. Then, by some miracle, the 49ers came roaring back to life and scored thirty-one unanswered points in the second half. They ended up winning the game 38–35 and setting an NFL comeback record.

Football Angels

Who was the sweetest, cleanest team of all time? The Detroit Lions ended the 1937 season with only nineteen penalties for a total of 139 yards.

The Brooklyn Dodgers may not have been a very successful NFL franchise, lasting only from 1930 to 1944, but they were polite. They are in the NFL record book twice for playing in games in which no penalties were given. The first game was against Pittsburgh in 1934 and the other against Boston in 1936.

Injury Immunity

Jim Marshall's NFL career spanned twenty seasons, and he set an NFL record for starting in 282 consecutive games. Jim did all of this injury-free, with not even a bump or bruise to keep him out of a game. When Jim retired in 1980, his lucky streak ran out. Instead of thanking his lucky stars and wrapping himself in cotton batting for the remainder of his life, Jim decided to push his luck by taking up hang gliding. Did Jim's luck hold? Of course not. Jim's glider was barely off the ground when he crashed into a light pole at a local school field and went crashing to the earth. Jim wasn't seriously injured, but he did cancel those crocodile-wrestling lessons.

Yank Me

I'm sure your sports guy knows the New York Yankees baseball team. But ask Mr. Smarty-Pants if he knows the other New York Yankees. There was once a Yankees football team. It was in 1946, and the New York Yankees pro football team played in the All-American Football Conference. Unfortunately, the Yankees couldn't compete with the drawing power of the New York Giants and soon folded.

Football versus Marriage

It was a moral dilemma. Duke Hanny of the Chicago Bears had planned his wedding for the 1925 season, on a game day. When he asked coach George Halas for permission to skip the game, he was denied. No way would the coach let him out of the game, and if he did miss it without permission, he would be blackballed. If he missed the wedding day... well... the punishment might be about the same. So Duke came up with a plan. He suited up for game day and lined up on the field. Immediately after the opening kickoff, Duke ran up to the first defender he saw and coldcocked him. The referee instantly threw Duke out of the game. Duke donned his biggest smile and best suit and went off to get hitched.

Spilled Blood

If you play any touch football in your family, you know how easily a ten-year family feud can erupt in the heat of the moment. Imagine if you were playing in the NFL with that good-for-nothing, cheating brother of yours. Here are a few brothers who have played together in the NFL:

Ted, Lou, and Alex Karras   Tody and Bubba Smith
Bill, Rich, and Ron Saul   Marvin and Gene Upshaw
Phil and Merlin Olsen   Lin, Walt, and Jim Houston

Super Bowl Slacker

Which player received not one but two Super Bowl rings, even though he'd never played a single regular-season or postseason game from 1977 to 1980? It was reserve quarterback Cliff Stoudt of the Pittsburgh Steelers. Cliff was the reserve backup for Hall of Famer Terry Bradshaw and sat on the bench for a boring three years before he had a chance to play in October 1980.

Playing Unprotected

Here is another one for Mr. Smarty-Pants. What NFL championship game has no official records, stats, or play-by-play?

It was the 1935 game between the Giants and the Detroit Lions in the University of Detroit stadium. The reason all the records were lost was that the game was played in the rain and snow, and the stands were unprotected from the elements. All paper and notes turned into useless, soggy, smeared blobs of goo after the game and had to be thrown in the trash.

Slip of the Tongue

We've got to give the sportscasters a bit of a break. They are yacking constantly, and once in a while they do slip up and get a bit tongue-tied. Sportscaster Curt Gowdy made the best, or at least the most hilarious, blooper during the telecast of an all-star game. When pointing out that a recent downpour had caused a huge puddle on the playing field, he told viewers, "If there is a pileup out there, they'll have to give some of the players artificial insemination."

I'm sure those guys would have enough trouble letting someone put their lips on them, let alone anything else.

Hot Pants

It was 1970. *Monday Night Football* was in its first season, and there were bell-bottoms involved. Play-by-play man Keith Jackson was bellowing through the airwaves when the incident happened.

You have to remember this was in the days when everyone smoked, and many sports announcers sat at one table chucking used wads of football notes around. Just as a brouhaha broke out on the field, a fire broke out in Jackson's pants. While still announcing the events taking place on the field, Jackson grabbed every cup around him and doused himself in liquid refreshments. The fire was soon out and, fortunately, Jackson was not injured. His pants, however, didn't make it.

"One of the things I do remember most about it now is that I sure didn't get any help from my partners. Don was cracking up and rolling around on the floor. Howard was jumping up and down and screaming for someone to call the fire department. I had to put the fire out all by myself."

With friends like that, who needs enemies to light you on fire?

There you go, girls. Start betting, make some money, but, most importantly, make your guy look like an ass.

college boys like to do it, too

THE GAME OF COLLEGE FOOTBALL

College football looks a lot like NFL football at first glance. Apart from the loose uniform rules in college that give us the occasional peek at exposed six-pack bellies, you'd never be able to tell the difference. Their butts are just as hard; their pants are just as tight and shiny; and the quarterback's teeth are just as straight and pearly white. But college football is a slightly different game.

College Football Facts

ORIGINS OF THE GAME

If Sunday afternoon and Monday night is for the NFL, then Saturdays belong to college football. In fact, the game of college football was officially born on a Saturday. On Saturday, November 6, 1869, when Rutgers took the challenge laid by Princeton for an afternoon game, college football was born. As we have learned in the first chapter of this book, the game of football began and evolved on college campuses. The NFL's rules, traditions, and evolution were nurtured by the college game. It took the professional game of football almost a century to match America's passion for college football. The college game offers a local flavor and more than a century of tradition behind it.

GET ORGANIZED

In 1876, representatives from Harvard and Yale met at the Massasoit House, a hotel in Springfield, Massachusetts. They were not meeting up for a cheap, lurid affair but to write some cheap, lurid rules to this new game of football and form the Intercollegiate Football Association. The IFA was the first organization to govern football and was headed by football's famous rulemaker, Walter Camp. Although the game they were governing was actually closer to rugby than football as we know it today, it was still the early form of our beloved game.

The IFA continued to rule college football until 1906. That year, the public began to raise a stink about the brutality of the game. The stink rose all the way to President Theodore Roosevelt, and the President decided to do something about this dangerous pastime on the campuses of America. He called representatives of Princeton, Yale, and Harvard to the White House. The President told the college representatives that they had better clean up the game to make it less brutal, or he would ban the sport altogether. It was a kick in college football's pants. Representatives from twenty-eight colleges that were not members of the IFA met in New York City to establish the new, cleaner rules and form their own rules committee. The new group was simply called the Conference Committee and was headed by Captain Palmer E. Pierce of Army. Pierce soon met with the leader of the IFA, Walter Camp, and the two groups decided to merge, forming the Intercollegiate Football Rules Committee.

In 1910, the IFRC changed its name to the National Collegiate Athletic Association. The NCAA is still the governing body over college football today. Though they started with football, the organization now oversees all college sports—men's and women's.

DIVISIONS, CONFERENCES, AND TEAMS

The NCAA divides the colleges into divisions based on enrollment, financial commitment, and the competitive level of the conference in which they belong. The NCAA wants a fair playing field; they wouldn't want a big powerful college playing a little college.

The colleges are divided into four divisions: Division I-A, Division I-AA, Division II, and Division III. The divisions are further divided into conferences (which, for some reason, have really weird names).

The NCAA holds national playoffs for the smaller schools—Divisions I-AA, Division II, and Division III. But there is no format for Division I-A. These guys settle their championships with those bazillion different bowl games that we hear about (to learn more on the bowls, see "How about a Soup Bowl," later in this chapter). We are going to generally focus on the larger colleges in Division I-A in this chapter because they are the ones that you will hear your football guy yack about most often.

In Division I-A, there are a zillion teams in a million conferences. Okay, I may be exaggerating. There are twelve conferences and a whopping 115 teams in Division I-A. Luckily, we don't need to know about all of these conferences and teams. I am just going to list the six most well-known conferences and the teams within them. They are:

The Big Ten (which, strangely enough, has eleven teams): Illinois, Indiana, Iowa, Michigan, Michigan State, Minnesota, Northwestern, Ohio State, Penn State, Purdue, and Wisconsin

Pac-10: Arizona, Arizona State, Oregon, Oregon State, Stanford, UCLA, USC, California, Washington, and Washington State

SEC (Southeastern Conference): East Division: Florida, Georgia, Kentucky, South Carolina, Tennessee, and Vanderbuilt
West Division: Alabama, Arkansas, Auburn, LSU, Mississippi, and Mississippi State

ACC (Atlantic Coast Conference): Clemson, Duke, Florida State, Georgia Tech, Maryland, North Carolina, North Carolina State, Virginia, and Wake Forest

The Big 12: North: Colorado, Iowa State, Kansas, Kansas State, Missouri, and Nebraska
South: Baylor, Oklahoma, Oklahoma State, Texas, Texas A&M, and Texas Tech

The Big East: Boston College, University of Miami, Pittsburgh, Rutgers, Syracuse, Temple, Virginia Tech, and West Virginia

Besides those teams, you have probably heard of Army, Navy, and Notre Dame. They head a group called "independents." Independents are the teams that never joined a conference. Because of the rich history behind these three teams, they have no trouble scheduling games.

There is one conference in Division I-AA that you should also be familiar with. The Ivy League was formed by colleges that do not give athletic scholarships and focus more on academic excellence. It includes Harvard, Yale, Dartmouth, Brown, Columbia, Cornell, Penn, and Princeton. Because the game of football actually evolved on some of these campuses—especially Harvard, Princeton, and Yale—these schools still attract many talented football players. The only difference is that these players are mostly focused on their academics rather than making it to the NFL.

While most of the NFL players are drafted from the bigger college teams that we have already mentioned, sometimes great players come from the smaller colleges. Walter Payton and Jerry Rice were both small-college players. Payton starred at Jackson State in Mississippi, and Rice was drafted from Mississippi Valley State (both in Division I-AA).

SAME BUT DIFFERENT

If you are planning to watch a few college games, there are a few differences you should be aware of. All major football leagues base their rules on the college rules, but there are slight variations:

- In college ball, the hash marks are slightly closer to the sidelines than in the pros.
- In college football, a receiver with the ball is ruled inbounds as long as one foot is inbounds (within the playing field). In NFL football, the receiver has to have both feet inbounds.
- In college ball, if an offensive player with the ball slips, falls, or even so much as touches a knee to the ground, then that player is considered down. It doesn't matter if a defender touched the player or not. In the NFL, as long as the offensive player hasn't been touched by a player on the defense, he can fall down, get up, and continue running as much as he wants.
- In cases of overtime, the two leagues also differ. The college game only uses the NFL's sudden-death overtime format in championship level games. Otherwise, a tie is settled with an extra quarter, and the team with the highest points at the end of this quarter wins.

College Legends and Lore

The history of college football is rich and jam-packed with legends. It has legendary bowls (who could forget the Alamo Bowl), legendary trophies (Memphis State and Arkansas State battle for a coveted paint bucket), and legendary rivalries (the Army and Navy have been fighting since 1890). The legends of college football are colorful, sometimes scary, and often completely silly.

HOW ABOUT A SOUP BOWL?

Instead of one national title game, like the Super Bowl, Division I-A has a bowl system. This is a series of matchups selected by bowl committees and the individual bowl's association with particular conferences. These bowls are held around the Christmas holidays and on New Year's Day. Since the first Rose Bowl was broadcast on national radio in 1929, Americans have fallen in love with bowl games. Each year, 500,000 fans rush into stadiums, and 50 million fans watch the country's top college teams play for the coveted bowls on television. And there are a lot of them to covet. The success of early bowls have inspired many to invent their own bowls, usually to try and cash in on the popularity of the originals. Some of these bowls have lasted and others have not. Here are a few of the annual bowls.

Alamo Bowl	Heritage Bowl	Orange Bowl
Aloha Bowl	Holiday Bowl	Outback Bowl
Carquest Bowl	Humanitarian Bowl	Peach Bowl
Citrus Bowl	Independence Bowl	Rose Bowl
Cotton Bowl	Las Vegas Bowl	Sugar Bowl
Fiesta Bowl	Liberty Bowl	Sun Bowl
Gator Bowl	Motor City Bowl	

And that's not all of them, but luckily we don't have to know them all. The most important ones are the Rose Bowl, the Orange Bowl, the Sugar Bowl (no, I did not make that one up), the Cotton Bowl, and the Soup Bowl (okay, I made that one up).

The Rose Bowl: The Rose Bowl is the oldest of the bowls and got its name from the famous Rose Parade. The Tournament of Roses Association thought a football game would be a lovely addition to its New Year's

Day festivities, so the first Rose Bowl was held in 1902 in Pasadena, California, and soon became a tradition. In 1947, the bowl made an arrangement with the Big Ten and the Pacific Coast (now the Pac-10) conferences. Since this agreement, the Rose Bowl game has featured the champions from those two conferences.

The Orange Bowl: In 1935, a Miami man named Ernie Seiler saw a chance to promote football and Florida at the same time; thus, the Orange Bowl was born. In the early days, the popularity of the bowl grew slowly. But don't worry, Ernie had another idea. He came up with spectacular halftime shows and parades. Soon, the fans flocked and are still flocking. The Orange Bowl of today is now known for its fanfare and great games.

The Sugar Bowl: Two more guys thought that a bowl was a great idea in New Orleans in 1927. Colonel James M. Thompson, publisher of the *New Orleans Item,* and Fred Digby, a sports editor, wanted their own bowl to be held on New Year's Day. Fred Digby even had a name picked out—the Sugar Bowl. Why? Fred wanted the bowl to be played in Tulane Stadium, which is built on top of a sugar plantation, so Fred bugged everyone he knew to try to get this bowl going. Finally, in 1929, the local mayor sent a delegation to the Southern Conference asking for approval for their game. They were rejected. By this time, the whole community was behind the idea, and it was too late to give up. On December 2, 1934, Tulane University's Green Wave and Temple University's Owl were invited to play in the first-ever Sugar Bowl. Yes, I realize how absurd that statement sounds. Can you imagine it? A bunch of owls flapping around, almost drowning in a giant green wave, all within a bowl of sugar. Silliness.

The Cotton Bowl: A sportsman from Dallas, J. Curtis Sanford, wanted a bowl in Texas. So, in 1937, he began promoting the first three Cotton Bowls by himself. He then turned the Cotton Bowl over to the Cotton Bowl Athletic Association who have kept the tradition alive for the past 65 years. Since 1998, teams from the Big 12 and SEC meet to battle for the Cotton Bowl.

Some bowls are like one-night stands: they come and go. There have been many bowls throughout the history of college football that were held for a year or two and then lost forever. Here are a few of the bowls that never made it and my speculations on why:

The Bluegrass Bowl: Everyone must have started pickin' banjos and having sex with their cousins, forgetting about football and the game.
The Gotham Bowl: Batman quit the team, and then no one wanted to play anymore.
The Grape Bowl: Granny wanted it back for the dining room table.
The Raisin Bowl: Granny needed it; the grapes dried up.
The Salad Bowl: People couldn't stop laughing at the silly name long enough to drive to the stadium and actually see a game.

TREASURED TROPHIES

There are many respectable college trophies. The best known is the Heisman Trophy, which is awarded to America's most outstanding college football player. The Heisman is named after legendary coach John W. Heisman and has been awarded since 1935. The trophy, for the nation's top interior lineman is the Outland Trophy, and it's been going on since 1946. The Maxwell Award began in 1937 and, like the Heisman, is awarded to the top college player. The Lombardi Award is for the top lineman, and the Davey O'Brien Award is given to the best quarterback in the nation. These are the normal, respectable, sane trophies in college. But not all trophies are so normal, respectable, or sane.

I guess silliness should be expected when we combine intense rivalry, college boys, and beer for a hundred years. Throughout the history of college football, many pieces of junk have been given trophy status and become legends. Two of the most famous are The Little Brown Jug (awarded to the winners of the Michigan–Minnesota game each year) and The Old Oaken Bucket (annual prize for the winner of the Indiana–Purdue game).

The Old Oaken Bucket is one of the oldest football trophies in the nation. While the presentation of the trophy dates back seventy-five years, the bucket itself is more than 100 years old. The bucket was found decomposing and covered with moss and mold on a farm between Kent and Hanover in southern Indiana. The Chicago-based alumni groups of both Indiana and Purdue, who I think were on a bender at the time, decided in 1925 that a traditional trophy for the winner of the game would be appropriate, and the bucket was chosen. A link on a chain with either a "P" or "I" is added to the bucket each year. When the first game ended in a 0–0 tie, there was a panic, but the two teams decided to attach an "I-P" link to the bucket. Since then, there have been forty-eight "P" links, twenty-four "I" links, and two additional "I-P" links attached to the chain.

The Old Oaken Bucket isn't the only old piece of crap that is played for. Southern Methodist and Texas Christians fight over the Old Frying Pan; Bucknell and Temple fight for the Old Shoe; and Gettsburg and Muhlenberg for the Old Tin Cup.

Teams battle for various other bric-a-brac.

- Purdue and Illinois play for an antique cannon.
- Wisconsin and Minnesota play for Paul Bunyan's axe.
- Notre Dame and Purdue play for an old shillelagh (a kind of Irish bat).
- Tennessee and Kentucky play for the Beer Keg.
- Kansas and Missouri battle for the Indian War Drum.
- Texas and Oklahoma play for the Golden Hat.
- Florida and Florida State play for the Governor's Cup.
- Washington and Washington State play for the Apple Cup.
- Army–Navy–Air Force play for the Commander in Chief's Trophy.
- Minnesota and Northwestern play for the Governor's Victory Bell.
- Minnesota and Iowa play for the Floyd of Rosedale Trophy (a bronze piggy).
- The Illinois and Ohio State winner gets the Illibuck (a wooden turtle).
- Northwestern and Illinois play for the Sweet Sioux Tomahawk.
- Wichita and Wichita State play for a dog collar.
- Memphis State and Arkansas State battle for a paint bucket.

QUIBBLING RIVALRY

Rivalries are steeped in the history of college football. Every team has at least one archrival, and sometimes several. Usually rivalries occur between teams in the same conference or teams that are geographically close together. Whatever the reason for the rivalry, it gives students, alumni, and locals alike a reason to rage and party. There are a few rivalries that you should know about. Keep in mind that I'm going to tell you about only a few of the famous ones. There are many rivalries;

sometimes it seems that no two teams can meet on the field without bringing up grudges that have been going on for three generations. This list will help you sound cool. When you hear that two teams from the list are playing each other, you can say, "Wow, that will be a good game. Those guys have been at each other's throats since 1923."

- Harvard and Yale: started in 1875
- Army and Navy: started in 1890
- Texas and Oklahoma: started in 1895
- Michigan and Ohio State: started in 1897
- Notre Dame and USC: started in 1924 at the Rose Bowl

College Fandom

Okay, girls, if you are going to try and pass yourself off as a college football fan, there are a few more things that you should familiarize yourself with. It seems college football fans are born with this knowledge.

THE NAME GAME

Many college teams have nicknames, and many college teams have the same nickname. It can sometimes be confusing. If your guy starts babbling about the Bulldogs, he could be talking about Yale or Georgia or Louisiana Tech or Mississippi State or Drake—or your in-laws, for that matter.

Among the major colleges, the most common nicknames seem to be Tigers, Bulldogs, and Wildcats. Auburn, Clemson, Louisiana State, Princeton, and Tennessee State are all Tigers. Arizona, Kansas State, Kentucky, and Northwestern are all Wildcats. Also popular are the Lions, Bears, and Eagles. Michigan are Wolverines. USC are Trojans (not the condom), and Notre Dame are the Fighting Irish.

These names make sense. They inspire images of wild beasts. But some nicknames don't make sense and inspire images of… blue hens. Here are some of the weirdest nicknames in the history of college football:

- Delaware Fightin' Blue Hens (do they lay feisty blue eggs?)
- North Carolina Tar Heels (it makes them stick to the field better)
- Wake Forest Demon Deacons (do the Monster Ministers know about these guys?)

- Ohio Wesleyan Battling Bishops (finally, someone to put those darn Demon Deacons in their place)
- Swarthmore Little Quakers (the only thing scarier than a little Quaker is a mini-Mennonite)
- Texan Christian Horned Toads (I didn't think Christians were allowed to be horny)

POWERFUL PAGEANTRY

If you haven't already noticed, one of the amazing things about college football is that it offers pageantry. Most campuses have tailgate parties, marching bands, and cheerleaders. But some teams are famous for their traditional festivities. Here are a few to know.

The Stanford and Yale Bands: These guys are famous for their bizarre behavior, outlandish attire, and wacky halftime shows (including organized moonings and group pee-ins).

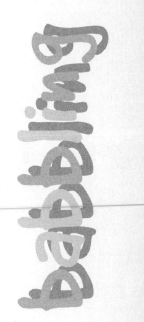

Dotting of the "I": The Buckeye Band ends every pregame performance at home by spelling out Ohio on the field, with the drum major running out to complete the spelling by dotting the "i."

Mascots: The best college mascots are the falcons that fly at halftime at the Air Force Academy, the live buffalo at Colorado, the bulldog from Georgia, and the creepy leprechaun at Notre Dame.

Notre Dame Victory March: It is said to be the fourth most famous song in America and the most famous fight song. And now, you can sing it (see "Notre Dame Victory March" on the next page).

SING A SONG

If you want to sound like a real football fan, you can sing a fight song. I've provided the choruses to some of the more famous ones. Shock your football guy by singing one of these little ditties in the shower.

Notre Dame Victory March

Cheer! Cheer for old Notre Dame
Wake up the echoes cheering her name
Send the volley cheer on high
Shake down the thunder from the sky
What tho' the odds may be great or small
Old Notre Dame will win over all
While her loyal Sons are
Marching onward to victory.

Rambling Wreck from Georgia Tech

I'm a rambling wreck from Georgia Tech
and a hell of an engineer
A hell of a hell of a hell of a hell
of a hell of an engineer
Like all good jolly fellows
I drink my whiskey clear
I'm a rambling wreck from Georgia Tech
and a hell of an engineer.

On, Brave Old Army Team

Oh, brave old Army team!
On to the fray.
Fight on to victory
For that's the fearless Army way.

There you go, girls. Now you know how college boys like to do it, who tells them to do it, and who they do it with. You also know why they would want to do it in a Sugar Bowl and what song you should sing if you catch them doing it. Now, get out there and do it with those college boys yourself!

canadians have bigger balls

THE NFL'S NORTHERN COUSIN—

CANADIAN FOOTBALL, EH?

Canadian football is a lot like American football, and at first glance—apart from the bleachers being filled with back-bacon-eating, tuque-wearing, extra-potent-beer-drinking hosers—you'd never be able to tell the difference. Then again, up until a few years ago, it was sometimes tough to tell the difference between the Canadian teams. Somehow, in what was then a nine-team league, two of the teams—Saskatchewan and Ottawa—had the same last name. The only subtle difference was that Ottawa was the Rough Riders (two words), while Saskatchewan was the Roughriders (one word). The Ottawa team folded a few years ago, leaving only one Roughrider on the block. However, there is talk in Ottawa now of reviving the team. Fortunately, potential owners have already said that the team would not be called the Rough Riders. They haven't explained their reasoning. Apart from the total lack of originality, I can't imagine why not. Perhaps because the name conjures images of marital aids or studded condoms?

The Canadian Football League teams begin play in June, and the season ends in late November (so the CFL season doesn't overlap with the Super Bowl). The divisions and teams in the CFL are as follows:

West Division	East Division
B.C. Lions	Hamilton Tiger-Cats
Calgary Stampeders	Montreal Alouettes
Edmonton Eskimos	Toronto Argonauts
Saskatchewan Roughriders	Winnipeg Blue Bombers

CFL Facts

ORIGINS OF THE GAME: NO WONDER IT'S CALLED THE "GREY CUP"

Canadians have been playing football almost as long as the Americans. As discussed in Chapter 1, the game of football evolved from rugby in the mid-nineteenth century. The Canadian game was influenced and modified by American football early in the twentieth century. In 1882, the Canadian Rugby Union was founded, giving the earliest teams a league in which to compete. In 1909, a championship trophy was established by the Governor General of Canada (the Queen's representative there), Albert Henry George Grey, the Fourth Earl of Grey. The Grey Cup was born. The first winner, in 1909, was the University of Toronto, and other early winners (with great names) included Toronto Balmy Beach (1927, 1930) and the Sarnia Imperials (1936). Since 1954, the Grey Cup has been awarded to professional teams only. The Canadian Football Council, which is now the Canadian Football League, formed in 1956 and became the governing body for professional football in the Great White North. For most of the years since, the Grey Cup has been won by the British Columbia Lions, Edmonton Eskimos, Calgary Stampeders, Saskatchewan Roughriders, Winnipeg Blue Bombers, Hamilton Tiger-Cats, Toronto Argonauts, Ottawa Rough Riders, or Montreal Alouettes. The CFL tried to push into the American market in the early 1990s with a team in Sacramento, California, and, in 1995, the Baltimore Stallions even brought the coveted Grey Cup south. But, by the following year, the experiment was deemed a failure, and the American teams were history.

THE CFL TEAMS: THE DIRTY DOZEN

One big difference between American and Canadian football is the number of players on the field. In the NFL, there are eleven per side.

Canadian football rules allow twelve men on the field. The more the merrier, I say.

FIELD... OF BIG DREAMS

With that extra slab of beefcake taking up space, the CFL made some extra room with a field that's nine meters (oh, sorry, ten yards) longer than the American field and eleven meters (sorry again, twelve yards) wider. The end zones are bigger in Canada too—twenty yards deep instead of ten. That's another reason why it's easier to score in Canada (besides the easy, loose men). Canadian fields also have a deadline marked off twenty-three meters (twenty-five yards) behind each goal line. This comes into play, as you'll see.

CANADIANS HAVE BIGGER BALLS

It's no lie. Canadian footballs are bigger than American footballs. The balls are more rounded and not as narrow as the American balls. And Canadians have white stripes around each end of the ball.

GETTING DOWN—CANADIAN STYLE

Another notable difference between American NFL-style football and Canadian football is the number of downs the offense gets. As we've learned, NFL offenses have four downs, or chances, to move the ball ten yards. In the CFL, they get only three downs. American football fans will tell you that's because Canadians get confused if they try to keep track of four downs. Canadian fans say three downs makes the games more exciting, since the offenses must pick up some big yards quickly. The system has actually made Canadian football a generally more high-scoring, offensive game.

SCORING IN THE CFL: "LA ROUGE"... ZEES EES WAHN POINT, NON?

Scoring is basically the same as in the American game, except for the single (known as a "rouge"), a point made when a team punts the ball over the opponent's deadline or sideline (touchline) in the goal area, or when the kicking team stops the opponent's kick receiver behind his own goal line.

CFL Crime and Punishment

There are a few rule differences between the NFL and the CFL. Unfortunately, the CFL doesn't allow bare-butt playoffs either, but we still have hope.

Men in Motion: You don't have to be some super special designated receiver-type man in motion in the Canadian Football League. Any player on the offensive line can be in motion before the ball is snapped.

Human-Tackling Dummies: In American football, a spindly little kick returner can save himself years of pain and aggravation by simply waving his hand in the air. It's called a "fair catch," and it means he's promising not to run after he catches the ball if those eleven angry men charging at him promise not to tackle him. It's a rule that makes sense, since a flea of a kick returner trying to concentrate on a high, hanging kick is pretty much dead meat. In the CFL, no fair catches are allowed. Ouch.

CFL Legends and Lore

PARTY ON

The Super Bowl is already just about the biggest party in the world, but thanks to a bunch of rowdy, horseback-riding Westerners, the Grey Cup ain't exactly a snore either. The party started in 1948, when men were men, and sheep were scared. The redneck Calgary Stampeders were to meet the city slicker Toronto Argonauts for the trophy, and the game was being played on the Argonauts' home turf—in the heart of corporate Canada. Under the facade of supporting their team, a bunch of crazy cowboys filled a few trains and came east to show Toronto how to turn a football game into a week-long party. They brought the world-famous rodeo—the Calgary Stampede—east with them. Riding shotgun on their train cars were some of Calgary's meanest bucking broncos and a couple of chuck wagons. The cowboys decked themselves out in white Stetsons and big belt buckles, and rode wild over the big city.

Fog Bowl

The 1962 Grey Cup has a place as the longest game in North American football history. Hamilton and Winnipeg were fighting for the championship at the Canadian National Exhibition Stadium in Toronto when a heavy, hazy fog rolled in. Fans in the good seats could see vague shadows moving, but those in the upper decks couldn't see a thing. TV cameras moved to field level, but with the fog getting worse, the game was called with 9:29 left. It resumed the next day, and Winnipeg held on to its 28–27 lead.

Would You Like to Use a Lifeline?

The 1950 Grey Cup was also known as the "Mud Bowl," and the sloppy, wet field almost swallowed Winnipeg lineman Bud Tinsley. Early in the game, which Toronto won 13–0, Tinsley collapsed face down in a pile of mud. Referee Hec Creighton rolled the big rookie on his back so he could breathe. Later, Tinsley said he wasn't drowning, but the incident led the league to rule that tarpaulins were mandatory for all stadiums.

Take Off, Eh!

There's a law in Canada that forces Canadian radio and television broadcasters to supply a certain amount of Canadian content on the air. Radio stations have a quota and must play so much Rush, BTO, and The Guess Who every hour, or they'll get their licenses yanked. Kind of helps explain Bryan Adams and Celine Dion, eh? Canadian football is no different, and CFL law allows only a certain number of Americans on each team.

The Record-Setting Stukuses

On November 5, 1938, a record that may never be broken was set. The three Stukus brothers—Annis, Bill, and Frank (collectively known as the "Stukii")—scored three touchdowns for Toronto against Montreal. It was the only time ever in the CFL that three brothers scored three touchdowns for the same team.

MAKE IT COUNT

In 1981, Pat Stoqua went the entire season without catching a single touch-down pass for the Ottawa Rough Riders. But after a dry regular season, Stoqua sent his team to the championship when he hauled in a 102-yard pass that sunk the Hamilton Tiger-Cats and sent Ottawa to the Grey Cup.

GEEZER'S STILL GOT LEG

British Columbia Lions kicker Lui Passaglia was in the league longer than many of his fans have been alive. Passaglia started with the Lions in 1976 and retired in 2000. Which means he's seen bell-bottoms come into fashion then go out of fashion then come back in fashion. He played through disco, punk, new wave, rap, grunge, hip hop, and tech-no. He even played through all five *Rocky* movies, all three *Rambo* movies, and one *Stop! Or My Mom Will Shoot* movie.

TWO-SPORT WONDER

Gerry James was a talented CFL player who also dabbled with sticks, skates, and pucks. Less than a year after winning the Grey Cup with the Winnipeg Blue Bombers in 1959, James switched to hockey and joined the Toronto Maple Leafs in the Stanley Cup finals that April. The Leafs lost to the Montreal Canadiens in four games.

AMEN TO THAT

Hamilton Tiger-Cats running back Dave Buchanan led the Eastern Conference in rushing in 1972 and later gave up football to become a preacher.

IF YOU CAN FIND A COACH ASS, HIRE HIM

The combined record of Saskatchewan Roughrider coaches Heinie Rogers and Jerry Crapper is a perfect 10–0. The two were Rider head coaches in the early 1920s.

OUT OF THE BLUE

According to brewing giant Labatt's website, their flagship beer, Labatt Blue, was named by fans of the Winnipeg Blue Bombers. The name was chosen because of the beer's blue label, and Bomber fans saluted their team by naming it "Blue."

SUCKY OR LUCKY

In 1981, the Montreal Alouettes set a new record and lowered the bar for underachievers everywhere. With a woeful 3–13 record, the Als somehow managed to make the playoffs as the third-place team in the four-team East Division. The pathetic Toronto Argonauts were 2–14.

SOMETIMES CANADIANS HAVE NO BALLS

Johnny Rodgers was a hero for the Montreal Alouettes when he caught a touchdown pass late in the game that iced a win. He got so excited celebrating that he tossed the ball into the crowd. When the teams lined up for the point after attempt, there was something missing… the ball! Rodgers had chucked the last game ball away, and there wasn't another to be found anywhere. The game was over.

FAMOUS CFLERS

Many of football's biggest names either got their big starts or spent some time in the Canadian Football League.

Doug Flutie: Arguably the CFL's best player ever, Flutie went north after a failed NFL career. He tried but never stuck with the New England Patriots and Chicago Bears after capturing a Heisman Trophy as the best player in U.S. college ball. He was famous before he ever stepped onto a pro football field when his miracle "Hail Mary" pass launched Boston College to a 47–45 win over heavily favored Miami.

After blazing up the northern skies, rewriting Canadian football record books and capturing three Grey Cup rings, Flutie returned south, where he kept his magic going with the Buffalo Bills. Flutie was sensational for the Bills and even had a cereal named after him—Flutie Flakes.

Then, for some mysterious reason, Buffalo coach Wade Phillips

benched Flutie in the 1999–2000 wildcard playoff game against Tennessee in favor of geeky, hand-band-wearing super dork Rob Johnson. With Flutie on the sidelines cheering his team on (like the little sportsman he is), the Bills had the game won until the final play. That was Tennessee's now famous "Music City Miracle" play. Called the "Home Run Throwback," tight end Frank Wychek tossed a cross-field lateral to Kevin Dyson, who ran it in seventy-five yards for the winning score with three seconds left on the clock. Who knows what would have happened if little Doug had played that game? Well, little Doug knows. He says the Bills would have won. Duh.

More Flutie Facts: Flutie's first CFL season was played in Vancouver, with the British Columbia Lions. That 1990 season was very un-Flutie, as he finished sixth in passing with 2,960 passing yards. By 1992, Flutie had signed with the Calgary Stampeders, where he established himself as a true superstar.

Flutie was named the CFL's most outstanding player in 1991, 1992, 1993, 1994, 1996, and 1997. He won the Grey Cup three times—one with Calgary in 1992 and two with Toronto in 1996 and 1997. Up to and including the 1996 season, Flutie completed 2,545 of 4,181 passes for 35,850 yards and 223 touchdowns. Flutie was the fastest QB to ever reach the 30,000-yard plateau.

Flutie owns dozens of other CFL records and holds innumerable team records established during his time in B.C. (1990–91), Calgary (1992–95), and Toronto (1996–97).

Flutie and his brother, standout CFL receiver Darren, are in a band, cleverly named "The Flutie Brothers." They considered calling themselves "The Roughriders" but thought it sounded kind of gay. Doug is the band's drummer.

Joe Theismann: The great Washington Redskins quarterback, who is now a TV analyst with ESPN, once chucked extra-large footballs for the Toronto Argonauts. Theismann moved on from Toronto to become one of the best quarterbacks in Redskins history. He has been an NFL and Super Bowl MVP, won Super Bowl XVII, and made the Pro Bowl (the NFL's all-star game) twice.

Warren Moon: The ageless wonder had a long and memorable NFL career with the Houston Oilers, Minnesota Vikings, Seattle Seahawks and Kansas City Chiefs, but, amazingly, despite his success south of the

sucky
sucky
sucky
sucky

hazy

border, his best years were spent in the CFL, where he threw many a touchdown for the Edmonton Eskimos. Moon reigned over one of the greatest football dynasties in Canada—and one of the great pro sports dynasties of all time. With Moon and the famed "Alberta Crude" defense, the Eskimos ruled the league with five straight Grey Cup wins from 1978 to 1982.

Pamela Anderson (or Pamela Lee, or whatever she is now): The world-famous superbabe owes everything she has to the Canadian Football League. She was discovered in 1989 while attending a British Columbia Lions game at Vancouver's B.C. Place. The bombshell caught the eye of one of the Jumbotron TV camera operators, who put Pamela on the big screen several times throughout the game. As fate would have it, Pammy was wearing a Labatt Blue beer T-shirt that night, which caught the attention of a Labatt bigwig attending the game. She was hired as a model, she appeared on some posters, and her natural talents led to *Playboy*, *Baywatch*, *VIP*, *Barb Wire*, and Tommy Lee. So there you go, girlfriends, you never know what can happen when you go to a game.

The Rock: World Wrestling Federation superstar "The Rock" was once an aspiring CFLer. The Rock, whose real name is Dwayne Johnson, laid the smack down at the 1995 Calgary Stampeders training camp as a defensive lineman fresh out of Miami. Alas, he did not end up with the team. Another famous wrestler, the late Brian Pillman, also passed through the Stampeder clubhouse.

The American Experience

In the early 1990s, the CFL tried to get a piece of the American pie by setting up camp with their southern cousins. The CFL's ill-fated voyage into the American south is but a blip in the league's rich history. But short though it was, the American experiment produced some great stories… and southern discomfort.

THE LAS VEGAS POSSE

The Posse had a short and not-so-sweet stay in the CFL in 1994, but their visit was memorable. They actually had some decent players, but the sideshow that followed the Posse was nothing short of ridiculous. Here's the rundown.

O Christmas Tree, We Stand on Guard for Thee: A national incident occurred when singer Dennis K.C. Parks mangled the Canadian national anthem, "O Canada," by singing it to the tune of "O Christmas Tree" at the Posse's first home game.

Way Offside: Trying to gain any advantage he could, Posse coach Ron Meyer asked the Posse Showgirls cheerleaders to hang around behind the B.C. Lions bench to distract the players. The Posse ended up losing the game anyway, but they continued to use their scantily clad cheerleaders to entice fans out to games by staging stunts such as halftime bikini contests.

Who Writes This Stuff?: The Posse practiced in a smaller-than-regulation field in a casino parking lot, where a sign read "Field of ImPOSSEable Dreams."

Cheap Seats: After crowds dwindled to minuscule numbers, all seats at the Silver Bowl were reduced to $9. The few who bought season tickets in more expensive categories (up to US$750) were given extra tickets to make up for the price difference. It didn't help—the Posse's eighth regular-season game versus Winnipeg attracted less than 2,500 people, many of whom were on casino excursions from Winnipeg. The final Posse home game was moved to Edmonton.

SHREVEPORT PIRATES: GOD SAYS SEND US MONEY... AND A GREY CUP

Though the Shreveport Pirates existed in the CFL for only two years, they are an endless source of fun facts. One of their many fans in Louisiana was well-known televangelist Jimmy Swaggart. Swaggart came up from Baton Rouge to watch the games, as he held Pirates season tickets. In an article just prior to the 1994 playoffs by Marty York of the *Globe and Mail*, Swaggart claimed that the 2–15 record the Pirates carried heading into their final game was part of the team's plan to "lull the league into taking the Pirates lightly," after which they would presumably make the playoffs and win the Grey Cup. Neither happened.

Don't Get Too Comfy, Coach: The Pirates are a prime example of how not to run a CFL expansion team. Team owner Bernard Glieberman and his son Lonie sold the Ottawa Rough Riders and set up shop in the bayou in the spring of 1994. Head coach John Huard was sacked two weeks before the first preseason game and replaced by Forrest Gregg.

Bubba, Was That You? Training camp was no picnic for the players. They were housed on the second floor of the Louisiana State Fair's livestock barn.

Bonnie and Clyde Revisited: The Pirates did not win a game in 1994 until week fifteen, when they defeated the Sacramento Gold Miners. The Pirates lasted through 1995, with an improved 5–13 record. By this point, the good citizens of Shreveport had largely forgotten about their pro football team, and it died after the Gliebermans could not negotiate a move to Norfolk, Virginia. Notable about the move to Virginia was "the Great Tucker Caper," when the city of Shreveport tried to seize Bernard Glieberman's 1948 Tucker for defaulting on debts related to the Pirates' lease at Independence Stadium. Glieberman's lawyer, Mark Gilliam, tried to escape with the car and hide the vintage auto, but he ran out of gas along the way. The police spotted him and took the car back to the museum where it was being stored until the case could be settled.

Canadian football versus American football. Yes, there are a few differences. But which is better? Which is tougher? Whose version is truer to the essence of the game?

Because I fear causing international conflict (and inflamed fans stalking me, waiting to beat me over the head with a tackling dummy), I will refrain from making judgments. Either way, football is a good game, whether you are a gun-totin', hot-blooded American or an igloo-dwellin', salmon-suckin' Canadian.

CHUCK:
For the record, that "gun-totin'", "igloo-dwellin'" stuff is Teena. I didn't say it. In fact, I love Americans and Canadians equally. Please don't show up at my door. On the other hand, Big Mouth is on her own and her number is in the book.

Conclusion

Happy Fandom

FOR MORE INFORMATION THAN YOUR

FOOTBALL GUY

So, girlfriend, I now crown you a football fan, a football chick, a football babe. You now know all you need to know to understand the game, and also why your guy loves it so much. If you thirst for still more football knowledge, or if you want to know even more than your football guy, here is a list of further resources:

The Official NFL site: **www.nfl.com**
More than you need to know about football.

NFL Players Association: **www.nflpa.com**
Want to see what your favorite player makes in a year?

The Pro Football Hall of Fame: **www.profootballhof.com**
Find out everything, and I mean every boring obscure fact, about football.

NFL players.com: **www.nflplayers.com**
Go see all of the cuties here.

CNN Sports Illustrated: **www.cnnsi.com**
Beat your guy to the latest news in football.

Football.com: **www.football.com**
This is a really good site for information on all leagues: NFL, CFL, college, and Arena. Also learn college fight songs here at **www.football.com/collegesongs/index.shtml**

National Collegiate Athletic Association: **www.ncaa.com**
The college football rulers.

Canadian Football League: **www.cfl.ca**
Find out all the details on the CFL, the Grey Cup, and links to all the CFL team sites.

Glossary

What's with all the jargon?

FOOTBALL ANNOUNCERS AND THE LANGUAGE

THEY SPEAK

From high above the playing field, up, up above the drunken yahoos in the nosebleed seats, waft the sobering, analytical voices of the men and women who know football best—the commentators. A play-by-play person tells you what's going on, and his sidekick, known as a color man, analyzes, informs, and fills in all the uncomfortable pauses between plays. But if you donta speaka the language, you can't absorb something like this: "Warner's calling an audible from the shotgun, he's got his wideout in motion, and here comes the safety blitz!" Spend the season training your football vocabulary, and by Super Bowl time you might actually realize that Pat Summerall and John Madden are indeed speaking English.

Alley-oop: This one probably reminds you of the circus aerialists who would chuck their partners up onto the top of a human pyramid and yell "Alley-oop!" It is similar in football. It is a long and high forward pass, thrown in desperation for anyone (preferably a receiver) who can grab it.

All-pro: An individual selected to play in the Pro Bowl game—football's all-star game for the best players.

All the Way: Now we're talking! I love this game! Actually, "all the way" is just football talk for scoring… a touchdown, that is.

American Football Conference : One of the National Football League's two conferences. The other conference is the National Football Conference. See page 57 for details. The league is split into two conferences to help organize schedules, standings, and playoffs. Teams from separate conferences meet during the regular season. At playoff time, however, teams from each conference play off (duh) to determine conference champions. Those conference champions meet in the Super Bowl.

Audible: That's when the quarterback changes the play and informs his buddies of the new plan by yelling out a heavily coded set of signals. You know, the "Blah, blah, hut!" stuff.

Back: As in running back, fullback, halfback. A back is an offensive player who lines up at least a yard behind the line of scrimmage and is responsible for things such as running the ball, catching passes, and blocking.

Ballcarrier: That weird furniture store manager who always seems to have his hand in his pocket. In football, it's the player who runs with the ball.

Ball Control: Talk to the furniture store guy. Seriously, it's when the offensive team keeps possession of the ball for an extended period of time. Hey, as they say, the best defense is a good offense, and if a team has control of the ball, they can't get scored on.

Blitz: Just like it sounds—a risky defensive play where players charge the quarterback in the hope of hitting him so hard that his kids will be born dizzy. Most often employed when the defense anticipates a passing play. Also called a "red dog."

Block: A move by offensive players to stop or interfere with the defensive players by throwing their shoulders or body at them. No hands allowed.

Blown Assignment: A royal screwup. A major FUBAR. A one-way ticket to Benchville. A brain cramp. A big-time boo-boo. A boner among boners. An embarrassing failure to execute. A mistake.

Bomb: The big one. An exceptionally long pass by the quarterback. Always a spectacular play... when it works.

Bootleg: This is a near-fatal move by the quarterback in which he conceals the ball against the side of his leg and runs for his life.

Bullet: Another kind of pass, although it isn't as long as the bomb. It's more of a short, hard, fast pass.

Bump and Run: My last three boyfriends. A quick hit or bump by a cornerback to a receiver as the receiver launches from the line of scrimmage.

Burn: What I did to my last three boyfriends' stuff. To badly beat a defender by scoring or getting away from him for a big gain. See "Blown Assignment."

Buttonhook: One of the few genteel-sounding football terms. It sounds as if it refers to something that Grandma would teach you to do, or a really cute turtle's nose. Actually, it's when a receiver runs downfield, suddenly stops short, turns quickly, and takes the pass.

Cab Squad: This is a funny term for players who are cut from the team but are kept around just in case. The story goes that the term came from the owner of the Cleveland Browns in the late 1940s. The owner was Mickey McBride, who was a taxi mogul. When a player was cut from Mickey's team, he wasn't sent packing but driving. Mickey would give cabby jobs to the cut players.

Center: The great big fat guy who hikes the ball to the quarterback.

Chain: A ten-yard length of chain used to measure the movement of the ball in a series of downs. When a team is moving the ball downfield well, the chains move with them; hence the term "moving the chains."

Chip Shot: A nice, short, easy field goal kick.

Clipping: A fifteen-yard penalty for hitting or throwing the body against the back of an opponent's legs outside the clipping-free zone.

Clothesline Tackle: To use the outstretched arm to knock an opponent on his butt, usually by smacking him with the forearm in the head or neck area. This move is so effective it has become a staple for pro wrestlers and sly siblings around the country.

Coin Toss: The method used at the beginning of a game or a sudden-death overtime period to determine which team will kick off.

Completion: A successful pass.

Conversion: A single point awarded for kicking the ball through the goalposts after a touchdown. A touchdown is worth six points, and after a successful conversion, it becomes seven. A team can also opt for a two-point conversion by trying to pass or run the ball back into the end zone instead of kicking for the one extra point. The single point is most commonly opted for.

Cornerback: A strong, fast defender who plays on the outer sides of the field and covers the wide receivers or defends against the sweep.

Counter: An offensive play designed to confuse the defense. The ball-carrier runs in the opposite direction to most of his blockers.

Crackback: To complete this maneuver, an element of surprise is essential. In this block, the receivers and flankers pretend that they are going to run a pass pattern, when suddenly they crackback and block the nearest linebacker.

Cut: A quick change of direction by a ballcarrier to avoid a defender.

Daylight: An opening in the defense for a ballcarrier to run through.

Deep Back: The player on the receiving team on a punt or kickoff who is positioned farthest downfield to catch and return a long kick. In other words, the guy who is far, far back when the other guy is kicking the ball.

Defensive Backs: The two cornerbacks and the two safeties who play defense behind the linebackers and defend against the pass or the run.

Delay of Game: A penalty against the offensive team if they fail to play the ball within a certain period of time.

Double Coverage: Two defenders guard one offensive player; a two-on-one scenario.

Down: One of four chances the offensive team has to move the ball ten yards downfield. Once they move the ball ten yards, they are given four new downs.

Down Indicator: Numbered cards used on the sidelines to indicate the ball's position on the field and the number of the down. Used in conjunction with the ten-yard chain.

Downing: Putting the ball on the ground to stop the play. Looks pretty silly.

Draw Play: A running play oh-so-cleverly disguised as a passing play. The quarterback, at the last moment, hands off to a back who then takes the ball and runs straight ahead.

Drive: A successful series of downs that usually ends in a score.

Drop Back: A quarterback steps back from the line of scrimmage to give himself breathing room to make a pass.

Eat the Ball: Sounds like the results of a terrible tackling accident, but really it is when a quarterback suffers a tackle and a loss of yards rather than risking a bad pass and possible interception.

Eligible Receiver: A player permitted to catch the ball—not all players are allowed to receive a pass.

Encroachment: Just before the ball is snapped, a player puts part of his body over the line of scrimmage or makes contact with an opposition player. Very similar to the game you used to play with your sibling in the back seat of the family car on vacations.

Ends: Two players on each team who line up at the outer edge of the offensive and defensive lines.

End Zones: The goal areas. The destinations. Jimmy Hoffa's final resting place. A ten-yard-deep area at each end of the field where touchdowns are scored.

End Zone Dance: The touchdown celebration. Many teams develop well-choreographed post-score routines. The more notable include the "Dirty Bird" dance performed by the Atlanta Falcons and the "Icky Shuffle" performed by former Cincinnati Bengals running back Icky Woods.

Extra Point: A point after a touchdown is scored. It's awarded for kicking the ball through the goalposts.

Face Mask: A penalty imposed for grabbing the protective face mask of an opponent as if it was a bowling ball. It is a penalty, but shaking the crap out of an opponent is still very satisfying.

Fair Catch: A catch of a punted ball in which the receiver waves his hand to indicate that he will not run when he catches the ball. Since he promises not to run, the kicking team isn't allowed to hit him.

False Start: A violation that occurs when an offensive player on the line of scrimmage moves before the ball is snapped.

Favorite: Of course Chuck and I don't gamble, but we understand that this is the term for the team favored to win by gamblers. In most games, one team is expected to win and is favored by a certain number of points. If the favorite wins by more than this number of points, they've covered the point spread and made anyone who bet on them very happy. If they lose, or win by less than the number of points in the point spread, anyone who bet on the other team wins. For example: St. Louis is the favorite over Tennessee by seven and a half points. If St. Louis wins by eight or more, and you bet on them, you win. This is a difficult concept to teach young fans. "We're cheering for Tennessee, Billy. We want them to win. Or at least lose by less than eight points."

Field Goal: Three points scored by kicking the ball through the uprights.

Field Position: The position of the line of scrimmage relative to the goal line.

Fifty-Yard Line: The midpoint of the field.

Flag: The referee's hanky, thrown to indicate he's going to call a penalty.

Flak Jacket: Torso protection worn by quarterbacks for their ribs and most of their vital organs (the jock is for the protection of the most vital of organs).

Flat: The area directly to the left or right of the line of scrimmage in an offensive formation.

Flea Flicker: Quarterback hands ball off. Ball is then handed back to quarterback. Quarterback throws a bomb. No fleas. No flicking. We don't get it either, but don't worry, it's a rarely used play.

Fly: A pattern by the receiver, who runs as fast as he can straight down the field.

Forearm Shiver: I like this one. This move is when a defensive lineman brings up his forearm like a club, and if it connects properly, the recipient "shivers." Not a good first-date move.

Formation: The pattern in which the offense or defense lines up at the start of a play.

Free Kick: A free kick is a situation where the kicker is allowed to punt or placekick the ball without the opposition bugging them. It is used after a touchdown, a safety, or a field goal.

Front Four: The two defensive tackles and the two defensive ends.

Frozen Tundra: A nickname for Lambeau Field, frosty home of the Green Bay Packers.

Fullback: The offensive back who positions himself behind the quarterback.

Fumble: When a ballcarrier accidentally drops the ball. Once the ball is dropped, it's up for grabs for anyone on either team. Don't tell the guy at the furniture store.

Game Breaker: A player capable of changing the course of a game with one big play.

Gang Tackle: When a few players gang up and tackle the ballcarrier. It's as painful as it sounds.

Goal Line: The line on the ground that runs the width of the field at the beginning of each end zone. This line on the ground extends upward as an invisible plane. A touchdown is scored when the ball breaks this plane, either carried by a ballcarrier or caught by a receiver.

Goal Line Stand: A furious battle close to the goal line, where the defensive team tries to keep the offense from scoring a touchdown.

Goalposts: The big Y-shaped posts in the end zone that are used in attempting field goals or extra point kicks after touchdowns.

Goal to Go: When the attacking team is less than ten yards from the goal line. They aren't looking to make a first down anymore, they just want to score. For example, if the ball is on the eight-yard line, the situation is first down and goal to go.

Gridiron: Just a cool name for a football field; based on the grid pattern formed by all the yard lines.

Guards: Two blocking offensive linemen who line up on either side of the center.

Halfback: A backfield offensive player.

Handoff: Giving, not passing, the ball to another player. It looks a little like "hot potato" on the run.

Hang Time: The amount of time a punt stays in the air. The longer it hangs, the more time the kicking team has to run downfield to attack the punt receiver.

Hear Footsteps: A pass receiver's loss of concentration when going for a pass because he feels an opponent closing in on him with the intention of beating the living crap out of him.

Hike: The center's snap of the ball to the quarterback.

Holding: A penalty in which a player on either side illegally uses his arms or hands to impede an opponent who is not the ballcarrier.

Hotdog: A showoff. An exhibitionist. That deep-cleavage wench who always gets out of speeding tickets.

Huddle: The strategy session where players gather round between plays to get signals straight for the next play. It takes place behind the line of scrimmage. Both the offensive team and the defenders huddle up. A good time to play "Compare the hard shiny butts."

Hurry-Up Offense (AKA No-Huddle Offense): A tactic employed by the offensive team, usually when trailing with time running out in the half or the end of the game. The team stops huddling between plays and rushes to start the next play right after the previous play ends. The quarterback will bark out the signals for the play from the line of scrimmage. This strategy also keeps the defense off-balance and tired—especially the beefy linemen.

I Formation: An offensive setup where two setbacks line up behind the quarterback and the third back lines up as a wide receiver.

Illegal Motion: Often called on bad dates; a penalty punishable by a swift stealthy kick to the jewels. In football, it is a violation caused by the movement of set offensive players at the line of scrimmage before the ball is snapped.

Incomplete: A pass that is not caught.

Intentional Grounding: A violation that occurs when a player intentionally throws the ball away so that it cannot be intercepted by the defense or caught by his own teammates.

Interception: When a defensive player catches a pass that the quarterback had intended for his own receiver. Also known as a pickoff or a turnover.

Juke: To fake an opponent out of position.

Key On: To focus on one particular opposing player and evaluate what he will do.

Kickoff: A ball kicked by the offensive team to the receiving team to start the play at the beginning of each game, at the beginning of the second half, or after a field goal or touchdown is scored.

Kickoff Return: The effort by the team receiving the kickoff to run the ball back for better field position.

Kill the Clock: To eat up as much time as possible by using running plays. A tactic by an offensive team with the lead late in the game.

Lateral: A pass in any direction except forward. The most recent, best example came in the 1999–2000 playoffs when the Tennessee Titans burned the Buffalo Bills with a last-second lateral that resulted in a game-winning touchdown.

Linebacker: A defender usually positioned a couple of yards behind the defensive linemen.

Line of Scrimmage: The imaginary line drawn across the field at the point where the ball was carried on the last play. This is where the action starts.

Loss of Down: A punishment to the offensive team, meaning that they lose a down.

Man in Motion: An offensive back's movement parallel to the line of scrimmage before the ball is snapped.

Man-to-Man Coverage: A defensive one-on-one strategy in which each player is assigned to stick to his offensive counterpart.

Meat Grinder: The area in which the opposition is very strong and in which your team is at its greatest risk. It is as if you (after having just come off a bad five-month Ben and Jerry's binge diet) and a really buff female personal trainer had a crush on the same guy. If you decided to go to the local pool for a swim, saw the buff bitch and your object of desire frolicking in the deep end, and then decided to approach the couple, then it would be said that you are "sticking your head in the meat grinder."

Monday Morning Quarterbacking: The American tradition of second-guessing a team's performance on the Monday following Sunday's game. Similar to the post-date report, evaluation, and interpretation meeting with your girlfriends.

Monday Night Football: A television tradition. One NFL game per week is highlighted on *Monday Night Football* for broadcast nationwide. Most other games are played on Sundays, with the exception of the odd Thursday or Saturday game.

National Football Conferencee: One of the National Football League's two conferences. The teams in the league are split into the AFC and NFC for scheduling and playoffs. See "American Football Conference" on page 57 for details.

Nose Guard: A defensive player who plays opposite the offensive center.

Offensive Line: Hey, baby, are your feet tired? Because you've been running through my mind all night. Screw me if I'm wrong, but is your name Zelda? Is your daddy a thief? Because it looks like he stole stars from the sky and put them in your eyes. I better go call heaven and tell them they're missing an angel. If I said you had a great body, would you hold it against me? Okay! Stop! That's enough with the come-ons. We're talking football here! A truly offensive line is five huge men who were poured into their uniforms to form a meaty barrier between their quarterback and the other team's bloodthirsty defense.

Offside: This violation occurs when any part of a player's body goes beyond the scrimmage line as the ball is put into play. It is often called on bad dates, too.

Onside Kick: A desperate move by the losing team to maintain ball possession while kicking off. The ball is kicked short to give the kicking team a chance to recover the ball before the receiving team. The ball must travel at least ten yards, though, so the move is a gamble.

Option Play: An offensive play that gives players the liberty to make a split-second decision to pass or run. There are quarterback options or halfback options, for example.

Pass Interference: A violation caused when a defender interferes with a receiver's attempt to catch a ball.

Pass Rush: The defensive line's charge against the passer.

Penalty: Loss of yardage or downs by a team that has broken the rules.

Penetration: It's not what you think. It's movement into the opponent's portion of the field. Hmm, maybe it is what you think.

Pigskin: Nickname for a football. Don't tell Babe.

Piling On: An illegal move in which defenders jump on a player after he's been tackled or had his forward motion stopped.

Pit: The main battleground. The trenches in the middle of the offensive and defensive lines—this is the real war zone in football.

Placekick: The type of kick used in a kickoff or an attempted field goal where the ball is set up on a tee or on the ground in a stationary position.

Play-Action Pass: The quarterback fakes a handoff then passes.

Playbook: The bible. A team's strategy and play manual.

Pocket: The imaginary zone behind the line of scrimmage formed by blockers in which the quarterback seeks safety from those big, mean defensive guys trying to stomp him.

Post Pattern: A pass route that sends a receiver downfield and cutting toward the goalposts.

Prevent Defense: A defensive strategy used late in a game by the team with the lead. The idea is to use extra pass defenders to prevent a long gain or a quick score, conceding short running plays that won't be much help to the offense.

Primary Receiver: The main receiver on a particular play.

Pull: Offensive blocking that sees guards and tackles pull out of the line of scrimmage and lead a running play around an end of the line of scrimmage.

Punt: A kick made by dropping the ball and then kicking it before it hits the ground.

Quarterback: The team's most important player and one of the toughest positions in all of pro sports. His responsibilities include calling signals and directing the offense, initiating offensive action on a play from the line of scrimmage, receiving the hike from the center, and dating the captain of the cheerleaders.

Quarterback Draw: A fake pass by the quarterback followed by a sprint up the middle of the field.

Quarterback Sneak: When the quarterback runs with the ball as soon as it's snapped to him. Often used when only a yard or less is needed for a first down or a touchdown.

Reception: A pass catch.

Referee: The main official who oversees the game flow by starting the clock and placing the ball in play. Head jerk.

Reverse: A play that is run in the opposite direction of the blocking pattern; a back moving in one direction hands the ball off to a teammate moving the opposite way.

Ring Bell: To whack someone's helmet hard enough for them to hear bells. This is also a bad first-date move, though sometimes deserved.

Rollout: An offensive play in which the quarterback runs out to one side of the field instead of stepping back into the pocket. Once he rolls out, he can either pass, run, or hand the ball off to a running back.

Roughing the Passer: A late hit on the quarterback after the pass has been thrown. What I often do to bad dates.

"Rumbling, Bumbling, Stumbling...!" A call popularized by ESPN announcer Chris Berman to describe a large man running the ball downfield. Usually used to describe a play in which the ball is fumbled and picked up by a big ol' lineman who isn't conditioned to run the ball but must when the opportunity presents itself.

Rush: Term used to describe either charging the passer or running the ball in an attempt to gain yards.

Sack: Downing the quarterback before he can throw the ball.

Safety: Two points awarded to the defensive team when they down an offensive player with the ball in his own end zone.

Safety Blitz: A safety's charge through the line to try to sack the quarterback.

Safety Valve: A secondary receiver who stays close to the line of scrimmage and is available as a target for the quarterback in case all other receivers are covered.

Scatback: A quick, tricky ballcarrier. The Road Runner would be a great scatback.

Scramble: A quarterback's attempt to make some yardage (by running downfield ducking and dodging defenders) after a failed pass play.

Screen Pass: A pass into the flat to a receiver who has some blockers in front of him.

Scrimmage: A play that starts with a snap of the ball from the line of scrimmage.

Secondary: The defensive backfield: two cornerbacks and two safeties. Their main job is to defend against the pass.

Setback: A back usually lined up behind the quarterback. What my therapist says happens to me after bad dates.

Shank: A flubbed kick hit with the wrong part of the foot so the ball travels only a short distance.

Shotgun Offense: The formation that sees the quarterback line up a few yards behind the center. The center's snap to the quarterback is much like the snap to a kicker for a punt.

Sideline Pass: A pass pattern that has the receivers sprint downfield and quickly run toward the sidelines to make the catch. The offense can stop the clock if the receiver makes it out of bounds with the ball.

Sidelines: The out-of-bounds areas running along the sides of the field. Along the sidelines you'll find the player benches, coaches, officials, reporters, photographers, and cheerleaders.

Slant: An angular run toward the goal line.

Sled: A training device used for blocking practice. It's a steel frame wrapped in pads that slides on the ground when players push and pound on it.

Slobber-Knocker: Coined by color commentator John Madden in reference to a punishing, but clean, tackle. When a ballcarrier is hit so hard something flies out of his nose, or mouth, that's a real slobber-knocker. Pretty gross to witness, even worse in slo-mo.

Snap: The center's hike of the ball from between his legs to the quarterback, punter, or other offensive back.

Special Teams: Squads with specific tasks such as kick returns, kickoff coverage, short yardage, etc.

Spike: To slam the ball to the ground after a touchdown. Can also be used by a quarterback who wants to stop the clock. He just spikes the ball into the ground directly after he takes the snap.

Spiral: The tight, twisting revolution of the ball as it cuts through the air on a perfect pass or kick.

Split the Uprights: The description of a successful field goal or point after kick that sails through the goalposts.

Squib: A kickoff that is both short and intentionally low to the ground, making it difficult for the receiving team to handle.

Statue of Liberty Play: A fake play in which the quarterback raises his arm as if to pass, but the ball is taken by a teammate behind him who can then either pass or run.

Stickum: A glue used by receivers to help them grip the ball. Stickum is now illegal.

Straight Arm: A ballcarrier extends his arm to shed tacklers. A useful maneuver in those "clearance sale" brawls.

Strip: To pull the ball from the ballcarrier, creating a fumble.

Sudden Death: Football's extra period of play used to break a tie. The first team to score wins. The nicey-nicey name is sudden victory.

Super Bowl: The big game. The National Football League championship that pits the winner of the American Football Conference against the winner from the National Football Conference. It's also America's biggest unofficial holiday and a perfect excuse to consume large quantities of pizza, chicken wings, and beer.

Sweep: The act of a ballcarrier following his blockers around the end of the line, rather than through the line.

Swing Pass: A quickly thrown pass to a back on either side of the field, roughly parallel with the quarterback.

Tackles: Offensive linemen positioned just outside the guards or defensive linemen positioned just inside the ends. Also, the act of grabbing the guy with the ball and slamming him to the ground.

Tailback: A running back positioned the greatest distance from the line of scrimmage.

Tailgate Party: A Sunday football game is more than just a game, it's an event. Fans gather in stadium parking lots early in the morning for barbeques and beers, and party right up until game time. It's a meat-fest in which you may actually see the reenactment of Fred Flintstone's car being rolled over by the weight of his order of take-out ribs.

T Formation: Forming a letter T, the quarterback lines up just behind the center, the fullback is five yards behind the quarterback, and the halfbacks are spread out beside the fullback.

Three-Point Stance: Player position before the snap: legs spread wide and one hand touching the ground, body leaning forward, ready to burst at the snap and start inflicting pain.

Tight End: The object of our lust, and the result of much heavy training and intense isometric butt exercises. Oh, it's also the offensive end who can either block or catch passes. (Note: All tight ends do not necessarily have tight ends.)

Time of Possession: The amount of time an offense controls the ball.

Touchback: A downed ball in the end zone after a punt or kickoff, which is brought out to the twenty-yard line for the first down of the receiving team.

Touchdown: Six points! Awarded when a team gets the ball over the opponent's goal line. A touchdown is awarded if any part of the ball pierces through the invisible plane of the goal line. Some of my girlfriends say their sex lives operate on a similar principle.

Trapped Pass: When a pass is thrown short and the receiver tries to catch the ball but partially traps it against the ground. Or any play that looks like a catch but the ball actually touches the ground before the receiver has control. The pass is deemed incomplete.

Two-Minute Warning: A signal that stops play with two minutes left in each half for an official time-out.

Underdog: The team not favored to win (also see "Favorite"). A gambling term referring to what should be the weaker team. If you bet on the underdog and they either win the game or at least lose by less than the point spread offered, you'll be a winner. Apparently this is a gambling term, but Chuck and I wouldn't know. Right, Chuck?

Chuck:
Yes, right. I'm saving all of my money for a minivan.

Unnecessary Roughness: Hard to believe, but all that crashing and bashing is actually well choreographed, and there actually is such a thing as a football player being too rough. If a player uses undue force, he gets a penalty.

Unsportsmanlike Conduct: Fighting, swearing at an official, unfairly assisting a player… anything contrary to good sportsmanship is punishable by a fifteen-yard penalty. I guess eleven large men leaping upon and crushing one poor bugger in unison is considered sportsmanlike.

Victory Shower: The ceremonial drenching of the coach with Gatorade after a big-game victory. Players grab the bucket as the game nears a close and pull a sneak attack on the coach. It's particularly invigorating in places such as Green Bay or Chicago when temperatures are below freezing. Coachcicles are always a crowd pleaser.

Waggle: So many butt jokes, so little time. The quarterback fakes to a running back (who looks like he'll run with the ball between the tackle and guard). The quarterback then moves wide and deep, and runs with the ball in the opposite direction.

Wedge: So many butt jokes, so little… never mind. A group of blockers who form a wedge-like blockade and try to make room for the kickoff return man.

Wide Receiver: A flankerback or split end in an offensive formation. These are the speedy string beans who line up at either side of the field, far away from the big, scary guys in the pit.

Wild Card Team: A team that makes the playoffs without actually winning its division in the regular season. The three best nondivision winners in each conference sneak into the playoffs as a "wild card" team. Baseball recently adopted this format, opening up the playoffs to one team in each league that does not win a division title.

Wishbone: A popular formation that has the quarterback lined up behind the center, the fullback five yards behind the quarterback, and the halfbacks behind and to the sides of the fullback, forming a wishbone shape.

Now you know all the lingo. It's like speaking a new language. The next time you want to describe last weekend's adventures in the bar to your girlfriends, you can say, "The first guy was a bit of a hotdogger, so I went for the meat grinder and rang his bell. The next guy to come in was perfect, so I blitzed him, then threw him the bomb. I knew that I was favored to win because I'd made the other women eat the ball. After a little fumbling, we had a completion. But when I got up for the victory shower, he'd pulled a bump and run."